Diplomacy under
a Foreign Flag

Edited by David D. Newsom

Diplomacy under a Foreign Flag

When Nations Break Relations

AN INSTITUTE FOR THE STUDY OF DIPLOMACY BOOK

HURST & COMPANY, LONDON
ST. MARTIN'S PRESS, NEW YORK

Copyright ©1990 Institute for the Study of Diplomacy
Georgetown University, Washington, DC
All rights reserved

Cased edition published simultaneously in the United Kingdom and the
United States of America by

C. Hurst & Co (Publishers) Ltd,
38 King Street
London, WC2E 8JT, England

St. Martin's Press, Inc.
175 Fifth Avenue
New York, NY 10010, USA

ISBNs
UK: 0–85065–082–9
USA: 0–312–04051–2
      0–934742–46–4 (pbk.)

Printed in the United States of America on acid-free stock

Library of Congress Cataloging-in-Publication Data

Diplomacy under a foreign flag: when nations break relations /
    edited by David D. Newsom.
        p.   cm.
    Includes bibliographic references.
    ISBN 0–312–04051–2 : $ — 0–934742–46–4 (pbk.) : $
    1. Protection of interests (international relations). 2. Protecting
powers. 3. Diplomatic and consular service. 4. Foreign offices. 5.
International relations. 6. United States—Foreign Relations—1945–
I. Newsom, David D.
JX1683.F6W47   1989
327.2—dc20   89–19983
                                                            CIP

Contents

Preface

AS A PART OF ITS OBJECTIVE OF FOCUSING ON THE processes of diplomacy, the Institute for the Study of Diplomacy seeks to illuminate specific aspects of diplomatic practice for academic, official, and general readers. This monograph concerns the procedures and problems that arise when countries break formal relations but continue to communicate—traditionally through protecting powers and, in a more recent innovation, through interests sections.

The Institute acknowledges with deep appreciation the J. Howard Pew Freedom Trust for its support of the conduct and publication of this study. The Institute also wishes to acknowledge the editorial contribution to this publication made by Margery Boichel Thompson, the Institute's editor; the design and composition by Jeffry A. Robelen; and the able assistance rendered by Kevin Briscoe, as well as by Joan Kontos and Taylor Fain, among others.

Article 45

If diplomatic relations are broken off between two States, or if a mission is permanently or temporarily recalled:

(a) The receiving State must, even in case of armed conflict, respect and protect the premises of the mission, together with its property and archives;

(b) The sending State may entrust the custody of the premises of the mission, together with its property and archives, to a third State acceptable to the receiving State;

(c) The sending State may entrust the protection of its interests and those of its nationals to a third State acceptable to the receiving State.

Article 46

A sending State may with the prior consent of a receiving State, and at the request of a third State not represented in the receiving State, undertake the temporary protection of the interests of the third State and of its nationals.

> — *Vienna Convention on Diplomatic Relations, done at Vienna, 18 April 1961 (entered into force on 24 April 1964)*

Part I

The Protecting Power

The Protecting Power

IN THE DECADES SINCE WORLD WAR II, DIPLOMATIC relations have become symbols in the conflict of nerves among nations. Wars are no longer declared. The deliberate niceties of "returning passports," once a signal of a serious break between countries, are seldom followed. Relations are broken on sudden impulse and with little ceremony. Nations new to independence, less traditional in their approach, use the gesture to satisfy internal political pressures or express a momentary anger.

This volume has grown out of the experience of those who have been involved in breaks in diplomatic relations and their aftermath. Its purpose is to familiarize students, scholars, and officials, as well as the general reader, with an important, if unusual, aspect of diplomacy: the role of the protecting power.

Ambassador James Blake, in the opening chapter, reviews the development of the practice, now universally recognized, of appointing another nation to represent an absent power in the event of a break. The next chapter, by Raymond Probst, former Swiss ambassador to Washington, describes the preeminent role of his country in serving, not only as a protecting power, but also as a mediator and arbitrator. The third chapter describes the Swiss role in representing United States interests in Iran and illustrates the special experience that Switzerland has contributed in such cases.

Breaks in diplomatic relations, described in matter-of-fact terms in news despatches, are difficult and often traumatic experiences to those involved. The fourth chapter describes such a break, that between the United States and Iraq in 1967.

The postwar period has also seen the creation of a new element, the interests section, in which diplomatic personnel of a country involved in a break serve under the flag of a protecting power. The United Kingdom and the Federal Republic of Germany were the first to employ this new device, the former after breaks with various states brought on by Southern Rhodesia's Unilateral Declaration of Independence in 1965, the latter in some Arab states in the wake of FRG recognition of the State of Israel in 1965. Part II of this volume contains four case histories by persons who served in interests sections, one in Cairo, one in Washington, one in Havana, and one who served in both Algiers and Baghdad. They convey the complexities of sorting out the responsibilities between the protecting power and the diplomatic personnel of the sending country involved in the break in relations and illustrate the types of problems encountered in such unusual circumstances.

In today's volatile world, the possibilities of breaks between nations will always be present. Even in such cases, as this volume illustrates, nations need to continue to communicate. The tradition of the protecting power provides the opportunity for such communication.

1

Pragmatic Diplomacy
The Origins and Use of the Protecting Power

James J. Blake

James J. Blake, retired U.S. Foreign Service officer and former ambassador with service in Europe, South Asia, and Africa, has combined experience with research to present the background to this study of the protecting power.

DIPLOMATIC PRACTICE AND INSTITUTIONS ARE THE RESULT not of theory but of the necessity for states to treat with each other in their own national interest on matters of mutual concern. Because communication is essential to diplomacy, states have devised over the years a variety of ways of keeping in contact with each other.

Among these ways has been the establishment of permanent diplomatic missions in each other's capitals, the Italians being the first to do so in the middle of the fifteenth century.[1] Summit meetings, attended by emperors and kings, and the use of special envoys are even older; both date at least from the Middle Ages. "Conference diplomacy" flourished after the Napoleonic wars, beginning with the Congress of Vienna in 1815, and was put on an institutional basis with the establishment of the League of Nations after the First World War and the United Nations after the Second World War.

The "protecting power" is but one of the many instruments states have developed out of the recognized necessity to maintain some communication with each other, however limited. Although elements of the protecting power's role can be traced to the sixteenth century and even to classical times, its contemporary form has developed only over the past century and a quarter, perhaps coincidentally with the vast increase in the number of sovereign states.[2]

A "protecting power" is a state that agrees to act on behalf of another at the latter's request within the territorial jurisdiction of a third state. The consent of the third state, either formal or tacit, is essential to the arrangement, which all parties understand to be, at least in theory, temporary in character. The protecting power and the state on whose behalf it is to act come to an agreement in general terms regarding the nature of the responsibilities entailed. Arrangements are also made by the protected state to reimburse the protecting power for any expenses it may incur in the former's behalf.

Protecting powers are often thought of in the context of two states that have gone to war against each other and closed their respective embassies. There are other reasons, however, why one state may ask another to act on its behalf as a protecting power. After the Second World War, some newly independent states used protecting powers in third countries until they could organize their own diplomatic services. The United States agreed to act in that capacity for the newly independent Republic of the Philippines in 1946.[3] Other states did the same in varying degrees for former dependencies.

Reasons of economy might also lead a state to ask another in the absence of a mission of its own to act occasionally in its behalf in a third country. Finally, a state may have recourse to the services of another in those countries in which its interests are modest and do not justify establishing a permanent diplomatic mission. For many years The Netherlands has acted in behalf of Luxembourg on political matters in certain countries, as has Belgium on commercial and consular matters in the same countries.

Historically, a few states have most frequently been called upon by others to act in their behalf as a protecting power. Switzerland has been among the most important, along with

Belgium, Spain, and Sweden. The United States has also had extensive experience in this area of international statecraft, beginning in the 1860s. In 1867, the United States served as the protecting power for Austrian interests in Mexico following the execution by Mexican forces of the Archduke Maximilian, who had endeavored to establish himself as Emperor of Mexico. Because recovery of the remains of the archduke was a sensitive problem for the Austrians, they chose to deal directly with the Mexican authorities, despite the presence of an American mission that could have acted in their behalf. Copies of the correspondence on the subject between the chancellor of the Austrian Empire and the Mexican minister of foreign affairs were sent after the event to the American minister.[4]

In contrast to the rather marginal role it played as a protecting power in Mexico, United States experience during the Franco-Prussian War was extensive. During that conflict (1870–71), the United States acted as the protecting power in France for several of the German states constituting the North German Confederation, which were at war with that country. (Switzerland acted in a similar capacity for several other German states).

Although he had little guidance from Washington as to just what was expected of him, the U.S. minister in Paris, E. B. Washburne, regarded his additional responsibilities seriously and construed them comprehensively. He stored the most important of the German archives in the American legation and raised the American flag over the German embassy, thereby signifying that the property was under the protection of the United States. He issued thousands of passports and visas to Germans who wanted to leave France, and he protested formally and vigorously to the French government when it initially prevented Germans of draft age from leaving.

During the performance of his duties, Minister Washburne rightly understood that he was neither the agent nor the representative of the German states in whose behalf he was acting. In disbursing funds he had received from the Prussian government to assist distressed Germans, he did so in his

capacity as "Minister of the United States, charged with the
protection of the subjects of the North German Confederation
in France, pending the existing war between France and
Prussia." He signed travel documents for Germans in the same
manner.[5]

The need for clarity on this point of "representation" was
demonstrated in 1871 after the United States agreed to a
request from Switzerland to extend protecting services to Swiss
citizens in various countries in which Switzerland did not have
diplomatic or consular representation of its own. When the
Department of State instructed the concerned American
overseas posts to extend such protection, it outlined what was
expected of them. Unfortunately, the instruction told the
diplomatic and consular officers that in exercising protecting
power responsibilities, the individual officer "...becomes the
agent of the foreign government as to the duties he may
perform for its citizens or subjects; he becomes responsible to
it for his discharge of those duties; and that government is
alone responsible for his acts in relation thereto."[6]

This "guidance" led several of the American legations and
consulates to communicate directly with the Swiss government
to ask for copies of its laws and regulations pertinent to their
new duties, for Swiss flags, and for the Swiss seal.

Bemused by these requests, the Swiss government tactfully
drew them to the attention of the Department of State. It
noted that in asking the United States to assume protecting
power responsibilities in its behalf, it had intended only that
good offices be made available to Swiss nationals who might
need them in the absence of a Swiss diplomatic mission or
consulate, and that it had not intended to establish what could
be regarded as Swiss consulates staffed by Americans. It
requested the Department of State to reinstruct the concerned
American overseas posts, and a probably somewhat embar-
rassed department did so.

In its new instruction, the Department of State invoked a
constitutional prohibition,[7] which has continued to figure in its
basic instructions on the protecting power responsibilities of
American posts. Under the Constitution, no person who is a

citizen of the United States holding any office under the United States may accept any office or title of any kind whatsoever from any foreign state or sovereign without the consent of Congress (Article I, Section 9, ¶8).

The department's *Foreign Affairs Manual* [hereafter, *FAM*] cautions officers as follows:

> In the course of protecting the interests of a foreign state, an officer of an overseas post shall *not* [emphasis in the original]:
>
> a. Perform any duty which involves the acceptance of an office.
> b. Display the coat-of-arms or the flag of the protected power or employ its seal or the seal of any of its diplomatic or consular offices.[8]

It was noted above that the scope of a protecting power's responsibilities are a function of the agreement it reaches with the state in whose behalf it is to act and the consent of the state within whose jurisdiction they are to be performed. They may vary from "good offices" only to more extensive services. The Department of State's manual notes that "informal good offices" could entail no more than the provision of "occasional visa and invoice services," but that "in actual practice" the distinction between "formal protection and informal good offices is difficult" [*FAM* ¶914]. "Good offices" or "informal good offices" might conveniently be thought of as limited, occasional services performed for the nationals of the protected state, or for that state itself on a specific problem. Local circumstances obviously affect the extent to which a protecting power may act in behalf of another, as do the reasons why the latter does not have diplomatic relations with the third country.

In contrast to "informal good offices," more extensive protection, according to the guidance provided to American overseas posts, could include the following:

—notifying a local government that the property of a protected state had been taken under United States protection;

—affixing the seal of the United States on such property with

a notice that it was now under the protection of the United
States;
—making an inventory of and storing the protected state's
property in a commercially reliable warehouse or repository.

Current guidance requires an overseas post to obtain the
specific authorization of the Department of State before storing
the property of a protected state on the premises of the post.
Posts are also enjoined from agreeing on their own authority
to undertake the protection of the interests of a foreign power
if requested to do so by a representative of the latter. All such
requests must be forwarded to the Department of State for
decision [*FAM* ¶921.2; ¶924.2 and ¶925.2].

In agreeing to act as a protecting power, there is no obliga-
tion that a state act against its own interests. American overseas
posts are cautioned, for example, against doing anything that
could be "detrimental to American trade or other interests...
or which might not be performed under the established policy
of the United States Government for nationals of the United
States under identical conditions" [*FAM* ¶924.2]. They accept
instructions from the Department of State, not from the
protected state.

Until the negotiation of the Geneva Prisoners of War
Convention in 1929, the extent to which a protecting power
could involve itself on behalf of the prisoners of a belligerent
state for which it had agreed to act was not only undefined but
also highly sensitive, because of the risk such involvement
could pose for its own neutrality. During the Boer War the
United States acted as the protecting power for Great Britain.
It soon found that the South African government was unwilling
to allow the American consul in Pretoria to transmit to British
prisoners of war any official communications or funds from the
British government. The South African government did agree,
however, that the American consul could forward letters,
papers, and funds sent by relatives to British prisoners of war.

No agreement was apparently reached on a proposal by The
Netherlands, the protecting power for South Africa in Great
Britain, for a reciprocal exchange of prisoner-of-war lists.

During the Russo-Japanese War such an exchange was carried out on the initiative of the French minister in Tokyo acting on behalf of Russia. This made it possible for the United States minister in Petrograd, who was acting in a protecting power capacity for Japan, to forward lists of Russian-held Japanese prisoners of war to the Japanese mission in Berlin. Representatives of the protecting powers were also permitted to visit prisoner-of-war camps.

A concern for preserving its own appearance of neutrality when acting in behalf of a belligerent can limit the extent to which a protecting power can press a host government. During the First World War, the American ambassador in Vienna complained to Washington that some belligerents on whose behalf the United States had agreed to act as a protecting power in Austria seemed to be unhappy with his efforts because they had forgotten that the United States had its own interests to protect in dealing with Austria. He noted that some Austrian officials were beginning to identify the United States with the enemy states on whose behalf he was so often required to act.

Sensitive to this problem, the Department of State tried to avoid involvement in prisoner-of-war issues when it acted as the protecting power during the First World War for Germany in Great Britain and for Great Britain in Germany. Under pressure from the American embassies in London and Berlin, the department eventually but reluctantly developed a program involving inspection by embassy representatives of prisoner-of-war installations in both countries on a reciprocal basis, to which Great Britain and Germany acceded.[9]

During the Second World War, as in the first, the United States was first a protecting power and then, after entering the conflict in 1941, a protected power. Greatly improved communications systems facilitated the various protecting powers' performance of the tasks of third-party representation. Nevertheless, serving as intermediaries between the multiplicity of parties to the conflict remained difficult, the more so because of the intense bitterness the conflict engendered.

The outbreak of war between Israel and several Arab states

in June 1967 led, for the United States, to a significant variation in the historical role of the protecting power. This was the resort to "interests sections" operating under the aegis of a protecting power.

When that war broke out, several Arab states severed diplomatic relations with the United States, which they identified with Israel, and closed their embassies in Washington. Perforce, the United States had to do the same in those Arab capitals, and various governments assumed responsibility for the protection of its interests: Spain in the United Arab Republic (Egypt), Switzerland in Algeria, Belgium in Iraq, The Netherlands in the Sudan, and Italy in Yemen. All of these third countries continued as protecting powers until diplomatic relations were restored, at different times, between the United States and the Arab states that had severed them.

The U.S. interests sections appear to have originated in the decision of several of the Arab states to allow a limited number of American personnel to remain in their respective capitals, following the closure of the embassies, to perform services as members of a "United States Interests Section" of the local protecting power for the United States.

In Cairo, as Donald Bergus recounts in chapter 5, these Americans constituted the "United States Interests Section, Embassy of Spain." The American staff, headed by a senior career Foreign Service officer, operated from the former U.S. chancery. Their premises were recognized as inviolable, and they enjoyed diplomatic privileges and immunities as members of the Spanish embassy, although listed separately as the "United States Interests Section" under that embassy on the Diplomatic List. As was the case with its Egyptian counterpart in Washington, which Ashraf Ghorbal examines in chapter 6, the section had direct, secure communications with its own government. In time, both interests sections enjoyed increased access to the host government and came to be regarded locally as something less than but approximating a diplomatic mission.[10] All this took place under the shelter of the respective protecting powers for the United States and Egypt.

As noted earlier, the host government has the right as sovereign to define the extent to which a protecting power may act in behalf of a third country. This principle was obviously applicable to the operation of interests sections inasmuch as they had no status independent of the embassy of their respective protecting powers. All of the host governments had the right to limit the operations of the sections, as was done in the Sudan in 1967.

As in Egypt, the Sudan had permitted a limited number of American diplomatic personnel to remain in the country after the severance of diplomatic ties with the United States. With the consent of the Sudanese government, these Americans constituted themselves as a unit of the Embassy of The Netherlands. However, in an exchange of notes with the Netherlands embassy, the Sudanese Foreign Ministry indicated that the interests section would continue to have "direct access to appropriate authorities...regarding commercial, economic and cultural" matters, but not on "diplomatic" matters. This omission was sharpened by the decision of the Sudanese government to permit the existence in Khartoum of an autonomous U.S. consulate that would continue to operate as it had before the break in diplomatic ties, with direct access to Sudanese officials.[11]

U.S. interests sections were also established in Algeria, Iraq, and Yemen. (William Eagleton describes the arrangements in Algiers and Baghdad in some detail in chapter 7.) Algeria had also permitted some American personnel to remain in Algiers after the break in diplomatic relations with the United States. They operated as a separate unit of the Embassy of Switzerland, the protecting power. As members of the Swiss embassy, the Americans had diplomatic status and their own communications with Washington, functioning without interruption from the former U.S. chancery.

It was not until February 1971, however, that the Department of State's *Foreign Service List* noted that the post "...is now referred to as the U.S. Interests Section of the Embassy of Switzerland in Algiers." The American unit in Cairo was first identified as "U.S. Interests Section, Spanish Embassy" in the *Foreign Service List* of September 1967; that in Khartoum as "U.S. Interests Section, Royal Netherlands Embassy" in the *List* of January 1969. The reasons for the different dates in the public identification of the sections reflected the evolution of U.S. relations with each of the three countries.

All American diplomatic personnel were withdrawn from Iraq and Yemen when those countries severed diplomatic relations with the United States in June 1967. Belgium acted as the protecting power for the United States in Baghdad, and Italy assumed the same responsibilities in San'a, the capital of Yemen. In the absence of American interests sections in their respective embassies, both governments performed the traditional tasks associated with the role of a protecting power to the extent that local circumstances permitted. A Belgian diplomatic officer carried out his duties from the former U.S. chancery, thereby indicating at least indirectly that the property was under the protection of Belgium. He remained in the former chancery until he was required, along with diplomats from other missions, to find new premises, owing to the Iraqi government's development plans for the area.

In 1972, a small U.S. interests section was established in Baghdad as a part of the Belgian embassy. A similar section had been established two years earlier in San'a as part of the Italian embassy and operated from the former U.S. embassy compound.

Despite the different dates and circumstances attending their establishment, all of these interests sections shared certain features:

—They operated under the aegis of a protecting power with the consent of the host government.
—They were staffed by Americans who enjoyed diplomatic status as members of the embassy of the protecting power.
—Their premises were separate from those of the protecting power and were recognized as inviolable, as were their separate communications facilities.
—They did not display either the American flag or the Seal of

the United States; office plaques identified them as U.S. interests sections of the protecting power.
—The scope of their activities and the number of their personnel were dependent on the host government.

All of these arrangements were reciprocal, with the United States according the same facilities to the Arab states concerned.[12]

As this is written, Switzerland acts as the protecting power for the United States in Iran, as does Belgium in Libya. In neither Iran nor Libya is there a U.S. interests section functioning as a unit of the protecting power's embassy. Agreements by the United States with Switzerland and Belgium define the scope of the services the United States would have the protecting powers attempt to provide. For the most part these services are consular, although the agreements specifically exclude the provision of visa services.[13]

The United States has not had formal diplomatic relations with Cuba since it severed them in 1961. After the break, limited contacts continued at a technical level in such areas as air traffic control and the exchange of information relating to hurricanes and Caribbean search and rescue operations. Any contacts at the political level were handled by Switzerland as the protecting power for the United States in Havana, including the 1965–73 refugee airlift, and by Czechoslovakia acting in a similar capacity for Cuba in Washington.

In May 1977, the United States and Cuba agreed to the establishment of interests sections under the embassies of their respective protecting powers and with the concurrence of the latter, as detailed by Wayne Smith in chapter 8. In announcing this development on June 3, 1977, the Department of State indicated that its purpose was to improve communications between the United States and Cuba.

Since then, the interests sections of the two countries have operated out of the chanceries of their former embassies in Washington and Havana, with the American unit identified as "Embassy of Switzerland in Havana, United States Interests Section," and that for Cuba "Embassy of Czechoslovakia in

Washington, Cuban Interests Section." The premises of both sections are inviolable, and each has its own secure, direct communications system.[14]

The United States and Cuba are not the only states with interests sections operating as autonomous units of a protecting power's embassy. Among others are a Soviet interests section attached to the embassy of Finland in Israel, the Soviet Union having severed diplomatic relations with Israel during the June War of 1967. An Israeli interests section is an autonomous unit of the embassy of The Netherlands in Moscow. Presumably both interests sections, and perhaps Finland and The Netherlands as the protecting powers, have facilitated the direct Soviet-Israeli governmental contacts that began in Helsinki in August 1986, the first since 1967.

In the mid-1980s, Great Britain, for another example, had interests sections in Libya, Iran, Syria, Guatemala, and Argentina. With the restoration of diplomatic relations between Britain and Guatemala on December 29, 1986, the British interests section in Guatemala City, which had been a part of the Swiss embassy, was closed. During the period of severed relations, Guatemala had had no corresponding interests section within a protecting power's embassy in London.

The British interests section in Tehran differed from the norm in that it was not the result of a break in diplomatic relations between Britain and Iran but rather followed a decision by Britain to close its embassy in Tehran. A small British diplomatic staff operated in Tehran as a British interests section in the Swedish embassy. Iran, however, retained its embassy in London, which was headed by a chargé d'affaires, not an ambassador. (In December 1988, the United Kingdom reopened its embassy in Tehran, only to close it in February 1989 in protest against the Iranian regime's call for the "execution" of Salman Rushdie.)

Because of its inherently limited, provisional role, a protecting power, with or without an interests section, cannot normally advance or promote the interests of a protected state as effectively as a permanent resident mission of the latter. The range of subjects a protecting power may raise with a host government in behalf of a third country for which it is acting is necessarily limited by the context in which it must operate, by its own interests, by diplomatic convention, and by the willingness of the host government to entertain certain subjects brought to its attention.

Nevertheless, the institution of the protecting power is recognized today as an instrument of international statecraft, as evidenced by the Vienna Convention on Diplomatic Relations (Articles 45 and 46), which was negotiated under United Nations auspices in 1961.[15] It has stood the test of time and necessity by proving its usefulness under a variety of circumstances. In accommodating the development of interests sections, it has also demonstrated its flexibility and vitality; and the sections themselves have often provided the basis for the resumption of the full diplomatic relations essential to effective communication between states.

2

The "Good Offices" of Switzerland and Her Role as Protecting Power

Raymond Probst

Former Swiss ambassador to the United States (1976–80) and former secretary of state in the Swiss Federal Department of Foreign Affairs (1980–84), Ambassador Probst has been a direct participant in the policies related to Switzerland's traditional role as a protecting power.

ONE MAY WELL ADDRESS THE NOTION OF THE "PROTECTING power" not as a singular contingency, but rather in a larger context. The performance of Switzerland in representing foreign interests is but an intrinsic part of her much larger vocation for providing international "good offices," which, in turn, stem from her traditional permanent neutrality. But what is the scope of "good offices" as we understand them, what does "permanent neutrality" mean, and how do these notions affect each other?

The term "good offices" as applied here, in a now widely accepted comprehensive sense, by far exceeds the precise legal definition of good offices, as well as the even more far-reaching notions of mediation and arbitration found in the textbooks. It refers, rather, to a wide range of diverse activities aimed at bridging the gap in international controversies, at smoothing out difficulties resulting therefrom, at peacefully settling differences or at least alleviating conflicts, and, in a more general way, at helping to maintain peace among nations.

It is surely no coincidence that neutral states are the ones called upon more often than others to render good offices. That does not mean that the ability to render such services is restricted to the neutrals. The possibilities offered to individual states by the "law of nations" for interceding in international conflicts are open to non-neutrals as well. A politically significant great power can also make use of this instrument and does so quite often—sometimes even by applying some pressure. However, in the course of more recent history, experience has abundantly shown that a neutral state, and even more the *permanently neutral state*, is in a particularly favorable position to assist other nations in coping with their conflicts.

Various elements inherent in neutrality contribute to this special ability. In the first place, to take the example of my country, the permanent neutrality developed by Switzerland constitutes in itself a factor of peace. Being neutral, she has clearly to abstain from involving herself in any conflict in time of war, under so-called ordinary neutrality, in conformity with the rules of the Fifth Hague Convention of 1907. Having opted, moreover, for a permanent—and armed—neutrality of her own, which has become part of customary international law, Switzerland feels bound to avoid taking any stand or measure, in time of peace, that could impair her status of neutrality should an armed conflict break out. As a consequence, the neutrality of Switzerland constitutes an element of continuity, of security and stability, which distinguishes her from other states that are only temporarily or occasionally neutral, and even more from those known as the nonaligned countries. The qualities of Swiss neutrality, by creating an atmosphere of confidence, are welcome factors for a lasting international cooperation.

Although the capacity to render good offices is not at all restricted to the permanently neutral state, a presumption of *bona fides* facilitates its intercession. This applies likewise to other neutrals, in particular Sweden and Austria. We look upon their activities in this field with much interest, since the positive steps taken by any one of the few neutral countries in the world forwards the potential role of all of them. In the case of Switzerland, the permanent and consequential nature of her policy of neutrality, her objectivity and impartiality, and her general availability for such matters offer a promising basis for possible success. Tradition, a long experience in international mediation, a favorable geographic position, an affinity with various cultures, and an understanding of their mutual relations are further helpful elements.

Specific Forms of Swiss "Good Offices"

Let us turn first to *mediation and settlement* of international disputes. Since early in this century, Switzerland has been repeatedly active in this field. The final phase of World War II gave us new opportunities to hold out a helping hand. The intercession of Swiss military and civilian personalities made it possible to accelerate the surrender of German forces in Northern Italy, thus sparing many lives, averting additional devastation, and preventing the planned destruction of Italian industry. Similar efforts of Swiss diplomats resulted in the surrender of the cities of Vichy in France and Bad Godesberg in Germany, without a single shot being fired, and, in Florence, in the rescue of persons and the preservation of irreplaceable works of art. In conducting these efforts, the Swiss diplomatic and consular officers involved could even draw special legitimacy from being at the time entrusted with the responsibility of protecting Allied property in the Axis territories.

After the war, Switzerland again did not hesitate to assume a number of *international mandates*. Among those entrusted to her by the newly created United Nations Organization were two important tasks that devolved upon her, together with Sweden, in 1953 at the end of the hostilities in Korea. Both countries were called upon to cooperate within the Neutral Nations Repatriation Commission to solve the question of the prisoners of war, as well as to join with Poland and Czechoslovakia in the Neutral Nations Supervisory Commission. Whereas the Repatriation Commission ended its task in 1954, the four-state Supervisory Commission is, to this day, still functioning. It continues to be regarded by all the interested parties, including the United States and China, as indispensable to the further implementation of a fragile armistice.

In another context, recent history has shown that definite benefits can result from the *granting of appropriate facilities to parties involved in difficult negotiations*. This was illustrated by, among others, the well-known French-Algerian negotiations held in 1961–62 in Evian, on the French side of Lake Geneva, which led eventually to the independence of Algeria. During the whole operation, Switzerland played a significant role— first, by carefully paving the way for preliminary contacts; then, in accommodating and protecting the Algerian delegation, which, for prestige reasons, insisted on maintaining its headquarters on the Swiss side of the lake; and, more generally, in endeavouring to create an atmosphere of confidence between the two parties. Excellent personal relations developed between the Algerian negotiators and the Swiss diplomats in charge of the operations (I happened to be one of them). The Algerians spoke quite openly with their Swiss interlocutors of the problems arising from the negotiations, asking them for their opinion and advice. Similar ties were maintained by the Swiss with the French side. This quite naturally led to a kind of unofficial interaction, thus efficiently contributing to the success of the negotiations.

Equally, Switzerland contributes to furthering international understanding by *extending hospitality to numerous international organizations*, such as the European Headquarters of the United Nations, the International Labour Organization, the World Health Organization, the UN High Commissioner for Refugees, UNCTAD, GATT, and many other governmental and nongovernmental bodies, not to forget the Swiss-created International Committee of the Red Cross and the League of Red Cross and Red Crescent Societies. Taking advantage of its excellent infrastructure, Geneva has acquired the position of a leading world center, as well as a secure meeting place for such important international gatherings as the November 1985 Summit between President Reagan and General Secretary Gorbachev or, as a more recent example, the transfer of the United Nations General Assembly from New York to Geneva in December 1988 in order to debate the question of Palestine.

Arbitration is another well-established method used to overcome international differences. It reached its climax before and around the turn of the century. Here again, Swiss governmental organs or individual Swiss personalities, being apart from the actual contentions, were very much in demand, especially for decisions of considerable practical or legal consequence. The international lawyer will recall the famous dispute between the United States and Great Britain in connection with the British armament of the Confederate privateer *Alabama* during the American Civil War,[1] or the cases of the Delagoa Bay Railway in what used to be Portuguese East Africa[2] and the 1891 incident concerning the attack on crewmen of the American warship *Baltimore* in Valparaíso, Chile,[3] all settled with substantial Swiss participation.

But the importance of international arbitration has receded as *judiciary settlement* of disputes gained momentum by the creation of the Permanent Court of International Justice of the League of Nations, reconstituted as the International Court of Justice within the UN system. However, the Court's jurisdiction is losing some of its weight. The reasons for this trend are manifold. The emergence of new states with different ideals and ethical principles of their own has shattered the previous homogeneousness prevailing over the family of states and has thus increased the number of political conflicts. Many of these states tend to reject the integral application of a Western-inspired international legal system, in the conception of which they had not participated, and to challenge preexisting international rules. Further, in certain instances, such as the case brought by Nicaragua against the United States, some major powers have refused to accept the Court's jurisdiction.

Nevertheless, Switzerland, which has initiated and concluded a great number of bilateral treaties in this field, remains strongly attached to the principles of arbitration and international jurisdiction. Its proposal at the Helsinki Conference on Security and Cooperation in Europe (CSCE) of a system of peaceful settlement of disputes, which was widely approved at Vienna in January 1989, bears witness to this constant line. The Vienna CSCE accepted a mandate for a further conference on the proposed system, to be held in Switzerland in early 1991.

Since the founding of the United Nations, the role of mediator has been increasingly assumed by the organization itself or by one of its organs. This has not kept the organization from repeatedly *entrusting Swiss personalities with special United Nations tasks*. The difficult mission successfully accomplished under heavy political strain by former Swiss diplomat Victor Umbricht in resolving the intricate economic and administrative problems brought about by the rupture of the former East African Community (Tanzania, Kenya, Uganda) is but one of the more recent examples. Nevertheless, the successive ascent of the United Nations to universality in some way modified Switzerland's role in the field of good offices, much of it now supplanted by the manifold peacekeeping measures of the organization itself or by its member states, mandated accordingly.

Because Switzerland is not herself a member of the "political" United Nations, albeit a full participant in the organization's specialized institutions and other "technical" agencies, her opportunities to proffer such services may have naturally shrunk. Things were not made easier by the Swiss voters' decision in March 1986 to stay aloof from full membership in the United Nations.

This did not, however, lessen Switzerland's disposition to assist this same organization in its peacekeeping efforts. In June 1988, the Swiss government, in response to a request by Secretary-General Pérez de Cuéllar, even decided to extend its participation in UN peacekeeping operations and to intensify its general efforts toward settling international conflicts. The dispatch in spring 1989 of a Swiss medical unit of one hundred fifty fully-equipped specialists (two airplanes included) in support of the UN Transition Assistance Group (UNTAG) in

Namibia gives evidence of this willingness. Moreover, some fifty trained Swiss specialists are to participate as observers at the elections leading to Namibia's independence, scheduled for autumn 1989.

Certainly there is still a predilection to call upon neutral states for smoothing tensions in the world, and there are still situations where some particular abilities, even of nationals of a nonmember like Switzerland, may be in demand. The nomination of Jean-Pierre Hocké, former director of operations of the International Committee of the Red Cross (ICRC) in Geneva, to be UN High Commissioner for Refugees is such a choice.

The Protecting Power Role

There is one domain, however, where things do not seem to change. Indeed, this brings us to the core of the matter: even as a nonmember of the United Nations, Switzerland remains the preferred *protecting power*. Why is this so? Switzerland's familiarity with the matter and her stable policy of permanent neutrality may be at least part of the answer.

And what is the task of a country called upon to represent the interests of a second state in a third one? Generally speaking, it consists in maintaining at least a minimum of contacts between belligerents or between states which have broken off their diplomatic relations for another reason, until hostilities cease or until both countries resume their ties. Basically, the protecting power does not function in its own name. Since it is mandated by one of the parties only, even though the mission has to be accepted by the other, it functions as a substitute for the first of them. Its actions are prescribed by the protected state and governed, moreover, by the appropriate rules of the law of nations.[4]

Accordingly, the protecting power does not, in principle, intervene as a mediator, even though, in the course of events, it could be led into taking initiatives of its own, such as in a period of acute crisis and extreme urgency. But when doing so, the protecting power will always endeavor to proceed within the guidelines received and to keep the protected state fully informed. Even some mediatory efforts, with the conflicting parties both agreeing, might be ventured. But great care will have to be taken, and much circumspection will be required from the protecting power, to avoid creating misunderstandings or appearing biased and thus risking impairment of its mandate.

Switzerland has a long experience in protecting foreign interests, beginning during the *Franco-Prussian War of 1870/ 71*, when the Swiss were entrusted with the interests of the Kingdom of Bavaria and of the Grand Duchy of Baden in France. During *World War I*, Switzerland acted as a protecting power of some twenty-five states. This type of activity reached its peak in the course of *World War II*, when Switzerland at one point simultaneously represented the interests of thirty-five nations, totaling some two hundred separate mandates. These included most of the belligerents and—of particular importance—almost all of the big powers. Moreover, Switzerland was often requested by both sides to look after their respective interests on a reciprocal basis.

Swiss diplomats took care of U.S. interests in twelve different enemy countries, among them the three Axis Powers, Germany, Italy, and Japan. Conversely, Switzerland also represented the three Axis Powers, as well as occupied France, in America. Such reciprocity not only facilitated the job, but gave us a handle for increasing our moderating influence. The same reciprocal channel was used in autumn 1945 for transmitting to the United States government the Japanese offer of surrender. We also functioned as technical intermediary in the subsequent negotiations leading finally to Japan's unconditional surrender.

Declining for a while after the end of the war, Switzerland's activities as protecting power soon gained new momentum with the growing international tension associated with the *Cold War and decolonization*. Since the mid-fifties, the mandates entrusted to the Swiss government have roughly oscillated between ten and twenty in number, among them the protection of American interests in Bulgaria from 1950 to 1958, as

well as American and British interests in Algeria from 1967 to
1973. The most eventful of these past mandates was the double
function simultaneously devolved upon Switzerland in December 1971 for Pakistan in India and for India in Pakistan
brought about by the hostilities generated by the separation of
Bangladesh from Pakistan. The tasks, including the eventual
exchange of military prisoners and civilian populations, were
manifold and heavy. Switzerland successfully insisted on
extending its protection beyond the ordinary diplomatic (and
consular) field into the humanitarian sphere. At the request of
both countries, she also embarked on a mediating effort,
eventually terminating the conflict. With diplomatic relations
being resumed in 1976, her double mandate came finally to an
end.

As of the end of 1988, Switzerland was in charge of fourteen
mandates. The protection of American interests in Cuba since
1961 and in Iran since 1979/80, as well as the British mandate
in Argentina since April 1982, are certainly the most promi-
nent among them. Let me dwell a while on these three cases.

The most enduring is our *mandate of 1961 for the United States
in Cuba*, supplemented three years later by the mandates of
nine Latin American states that also broke their relations with
Havana. The American mandate has now lasted for over a
quarter of a century. It had been a burdensome task, with ups
and downs, unexpected developments, and sudden changes of
scenery. There were numerous hijacked American airplanes
with passengers and crews to be taken care of and repatriated;
negotiations to be held on fisheries in the adjacent Caribbean
Sea, as well as on the prevention of sea and air piracy; and
many other tensions and complications, all constantly over-
shadowed by sometimes critical international tensions. To get
into all of these intricacies would require a separate presenta-
tion. Just one example, though, which I witnessed, was the
spectacular airlift between Varadero and Miami, instigated by
the Swiss in 1965, that enabled more than 260,000 Cubans
opposing the regime to emigrate to the United States over a
period of seven years.

A basic change finally took place in May 1977 when Washington and Havana each agreed to admit ten diplomats from the other side to their respective capitals. Accordingly, the American officers were integrated into the "United States Interests Section" of the Swiss embassy in Havana and enabled thenceforth to perform their duties in an eminently independent way. Switzerland has retained its status of protecting power, and its chief of mission remains ready for exceptional circumstances. The same applies reciprocally to the Cuban interests section within the Czechoslovakian Embassy in Washington.

Let us now turn to Switzerland's role in the *Iran hostage crisis*. It is not easy to add anything new to all that has already been published by so many others in the aftermath of those events. I would like, however, to call attention to the reports of two high State Department officials deeply involved in the issue who were particularly close to the Swiss team called upon to deal with the matter at the Embassy of Switzerland in Washington. The two were Under Secretary of State for Political Affairs David D. Newsom and Assistant Secretary for Near East and South Asia Harold H. Saunders, who headed the Iran Working Group during the crisis. David Newsom's article [see chapter 3] is essentially devoted to the Swiss role, the "sensitive link," as he calls it, in the U.S.–Iran hostage crisis.[5] Harold Saunders places the part played by the Swiss, appropriately, within the larger context of the American diplomatic efforts as a whole.[6] Indeed, a very close relationship, built on mutual trust and almost day-to-day cooperation during the most crucial phases had developed between us all. The events in question being thus widely publicized, I shall confine myself to some supplementary indications as perceived from the Swiss angle.

As early as November 1979, just shortly after the seizure of the American embassy hostages in Tehran and the occupation of the embassy compound, the American government approached Switzerland via the author, then ambassador of Switzerland to the United States, asking for his country's informal support in Tehran. It was immediately granted. During the next five months, Switzerland was discreetly acting as a kind of *de facto* caretaker. Indeed, diplomatic relations between the United States and Iran were not yet severed. The Iranian embassy in Washington continued to exist even though the American embassy in Tehran could no longer function.

First, a channel had to be established, beginning in Washington, going through the Federal Department of Foreign Affairs in Berne, and ending at the Swiss embassy in the Iranian capital. This channel served to transmit urgent messages and situation reports back and forth. Moreover, the Swiss authorities were able to arrange for secret contacts through their embassies in both countries, and even for top-secret meetings on Swiss territory of emissaries from both sides. Before and afterwards, the concern for the fate of the hostages was always on everybody's mind.

When these negotiations, which had appeared quite promising for a certain time, finally broke down in the face of internal Iranian antagonisms, the United States decided after all to formally break relations with Iran. It then requested Switzerland officially to take charge of its interests. Iran, for its part, entrusted Algeria with the protection of its interests in Washington. It was a lucky coincidence that the Algerian ambassador to the United States turned out to be an old acquaintance from the days of the Evian negotiations. Thus, we were soon able to establish a useful and trustful collaboration. The two mandates became simultaneously effective precisely on the day the United States chose to launch its abortive military operation to free the hostages.

After this catastrophe, delicate rapprochements, as well as long and persevering negotiations through different channels, were required before the release of the hostages was ultimately agreed towards the very end of 1980. As will be recalled, the Algerians were the ones who succeeded in achieving the decisive breakthrough, opening the way for the final bargaining by Deputy Secretary of State Warren Christopher on the American side. We sincerely congratulated our Algerian colleagues for this accomplishment. A solution had become especially difficult when already partitioned power structures in Tehran began increasingly shifting away from the Western-educated team supporting President Abolhassan Bani-Sadr to the religious fundamentalists, who had their intellectual roots in a totally different world. Therefore, the Algerians, as brothers in faith, and benefitting from their revolutionary past, appeared as more acceptable and credible mediators.

For her own part, Switzerland untiringly pursued her task of protecting American interests in Iran. She was able to better the lot of the hostages during their ordeal, holding a protecting hand over the American chargé d'affaires and his two companions, held in semi-captivity at the Ministry of Foreign Affairs; to repatriate the bodies of the eight unfortunate soldiers killed in the attempted liberation; and to organize the early return of a gravely ill hostage. She also succeeded in obtaining the release of, among others, an American journalist detained in Iran. At the present time, the Swiss embassy in Tehran continues taking care of a number of American-Iranian dual-nationals remaining in Iran and fulfilling all the other duties and chores pertaining to her task.

The mandate entrusted to Switzerland by the United Kingdom at the outbreak of *the Falkland/Malvinas Islands conflict* is the most recent among those still valid to this day. As often happens in such cases, the British request to take care of their interests in Argentina, forwarded through the intermediary of the Swiss ambassador in London, reached Berne on Friday, April 2, 1982, just before the weekend, late in the afternoon after office hours. Fortunately, President Fritz Honegger, Foreign Minister Pierre Aubert, Ambassador Edouard Brunner (my then deputy and future successor as State Secretary), and myself happened to be staying late at our desks. Since it was still around noon in Buenos Aires, we could immediately call our ambassador there, who had then to obtain the consent of the Argentine government. Everything worked out perfectly, and in less than two hours the Swiss embassy officials were able to take over the new task entrusted to them.

Needless to say, this task was not an easy one. We had to take charge of a huge embassy and two consulates general and assume the protection of thirty thousand British subjects (thirteen thousand of them dual nationals). The interests of the British subjects on the Falklands were not included, since the islands continued to be considered by London as British territory. We also had to organize the repatriation of the British diplomats, as well as a number of journalists, increase our own embassy staff, and assume many other duties pertaining to the mandate. Handling such administrative matters was facilitated by a mutual agreement permitting four diplomatic and four consular officers of each of the conflicting parties to remain on the spot at the disposal of the protecting diplomatic mission, i.e., the Swiss embassy in Buenos Aires and the Embassy of Brazil in London, mandated by Argentina. Assuring liaison between the two governments, however, remained the exclusive prerogative of the protecting powers.

The subsequent eruption of actual fighting additionally increased the burden, as well as the level of responsibility. Complementing the essential function of the International Committee of the Red Cross in Geneva for the protection of military personnel and civilians in the combat zone, Switzerland also had to play a supporting role in accelerating the eventual repatriation of the prisoners of war (essentially, the more than ten thousand Argentine military personnel captured on the islands). Since the hostilities ended, things have calmed down. The mandate remains, however, and the everyday tasks must still be dispatched. Switzerland continues to fulfill them to the best of her ability and for the benefit of both sides.

Just one further remark. It would be wrong to assume that Switzerland, as a Western country, is entrusted only with Western mandates. In fact, notwithstanding the U.S. mandate in Iran, Switzerland also represents Iranian interests in Egypt and South Africa, as well as South African matters in Iran. It was briefly in charge, in 1984, of Lebanese interests in Iran. Until recently, moreover, Switzerland functioned as protecting power for Côte d'Ivoire in Israel, for Yugoslavia in Morocco, and for Poland in Chile.

There are many other avenues for Switzerland to dispense her good offices. In most of the past, we undertook these tasks alone. Lately, we tend increasingly, in some fields, to work together with other nations who share our attitude or who adhere to views related to our own. I am in particular alluding to Swiss efforts within the *CSCE, the Conference on Security and Cooperation in Europe*, where, since 1972, we have joined forces first with our neutral friends from Austria, Sweden, and Finland, then with the nonaligned European countries. What might have appeared in the beginning as a fortuitous concurrence of disposition, successively developed into a fairly steady, continuous cooperation, with the mutual goal of maintaining and furthering the dialogue between the two parts of our divided European continent and, on a larger scale, between East and West in general. Certainly the "Neutrals and Nonaligned" (the so-called N+N) have not developed, and do not intend to develop, into a third European bloc. Two are more than enough. But they have, I suggest, been instrumental, again and again, with their suggestions, proposals, and initiatives, in helping to bridge the gap.

Finally, as a country sticking to its traditional permanent neutrality, Switzerland is not only qualified to render good offices and to step in as protecting power; it is *available* to do so. This is generally acknowledged by the family of nations. But it is not the Swiss habit to tender for such mandates. Whenever Switzerland's services are required, provided they do not hurt her vital interests, the matter will be favorably considered.

3

The Sensitive Link
The Swiss Role in the
U.S.–Iran Hostage Crisis

David D. Newsom

David D. Newsom, former Foreign Service officer, ambassador, and under secretary of state, held the latter position during the Iran hostage crisis and observed at first hand the role of the Swiss in protecting the interests of the United States in that crisis.

DURING THE LONG DAYS OF 1980, WHEN FIFTY-TWO OF MY diplomatic colleagues were held hostage in Iran, it was my custom to take an early morning walk. My route passed the Swiss embassy only a few blocks away. Each day as I passed, I could not help looking up at a window on the second floor— the office of the ambassador. Frequently a light would be burning at five or six in the morning. I knew that the ambassador was at work. I went to my own office with a special anticipation. That light suggested that our sensitive link with Iran, Ambassador Raymond Probst, had a new message, possibly of hope, possibly of disappointment. Beginning in April 1980, the Government of Switzerland formally represented U.S. interests in Iran, after assisting in other ways for the previous five months.

An earlier version of this chapter was originally prepared for a special volume of the Swiss Department of Foreign Affairs (see note 5, chapter 2).

Throughout those days Ambassador Probst played a critical role as communicator, counselor, and friend to those of us struggling with the frustration and impenetrability of postrevolutionary Iran. He became to those of us involved in the issue a symbol of extraordinary help to a friendly nation facing a serious crisis abroad.

Ambassador Probst, ably assisted by his minister Franz Muheim, was our link to his colleague in the Swiss Department of Foreign Affairs, Ambassador Edouard Brunner, and, to the end of the chain in Iran, Ambassador Erik Lang. All brought diplomatic skill, political perception, and sensitivity to the circumstances on both sides as they faced the special problems of dealing with the hostage question. It was my pleasure to deal with Ambassador Probst on an almost daily basis for fourteen months. I came to admire his special talents and, through him, the unique contribution that Switzerland makes to the management of international disputes.

The story began on November 4, 1979. Nearly a year had passed since an Islamic revolution led by the Ayatollah Khomeini had overthrown the government of Shah Reza Pahlevi. The government of the Shah had been strongly supported by the United States, and in the minds of the revolutionary leaders the United States shared in the responsibility for the alleged sins of the previous government.

The American embassy was located in a large compound in the center of Tehran. To many in the revolution it represented a hated symbol of the past relationship with the Shah's government. Already once before, on February 14, the embassy had been overrun and briefly occupied by militants supporting the revolution. The prime minister and foreign minister of Iran at the time, Mehdi Bazargan and Ibrahim Yazdi, had been instrumental in recovering the compound. Although most private American citizens had been evacuated from the country, the government of the United States considered it important to rebuild a relationship with this strategically located nation. Consequently, in the months between February and November 1979 there had been a slow rebuilding of the personnel of the embassy and at the same time some strengthening of its security arrangements.

Prior to his leaving Iran, the deposed Shah had spoken of going to the United States. The U.S. government had at that time agreed. The Shah, however, chose to remain nearer to Iran and proceeded first to Egypt and then to Morocco. As the influence of the Islamic revolution grew in the Arab world, the government of Morocco became increasingly uncomfortable with the presence of the Shah and he was asked to leave. Because of the delicacy of U.S. relations with the revolutionary government in Tehran, the United States did not agree to his entering the United States for permanent residence. He sought residence elsewhere and subsequently went to Mexico.

In mid-September the United States government began to receive reports that the Shah might be seriously ill. In October doctors were sent to examine the Shah, and a request was made to admit him to the United States for diagnosis and temporary treatment. It was revealed that the Shah had been suffering from lymph cancer for more than two years. Faced with what was seen as a humanitarian appeal from someone who had been a friend of the United States, President Carter agreed to the admission of the Shah and he entered the United States on October 22.

In subsequent conversations with Bruce Laingen, the U.S. chargé d'affaires, the Government of Iran expressed its strong disapproval of this act and requested assurances from the United States that the stay would be temporary. Those in the revolution clearly were fearful that the Shah's admission was but a pretext for a more permanent stay. Iranian leaders were apprehensive that the Shah, backed by the United States, would seek to overthrow the new government. The United States sought to assure Iran on this point and to share information on the Shah's medical condition although a request for Iranian doctors to examine the Shah was turned down.

The first hint of a stronger reaction came in a speech that Khomeini gave on October 28, which included this statement: "All our problems come from America. All the problems of Muslims stem from America—from an America that has strengthened Zionism to such an extent and is strengthening to such an extent that it is massacring our brothers in their multitudes."

Within days, Tehran radio broadcast instructions for a demonstration and a march on the United States Embassy. The march took place on November 1, but was kept away from proximity to the embassy by Iranian police. Three days later, the police were unable to divert another march and the embassy was overrun and those within the embassy taken hostage.

Three officers of the embassy, including Chargé d'Affaires Laingen, a political officer, Victor Thomseth, and a security officer, Michael Howland, were at the Ministry of Foreign Affairs when the embassy was overrun. They remained at the ministry, in telephone contact with the United States and in contact with Foreign Minister Yazdi. Laingen clearly hoped that the foreign minister and the prime minister would once more be able to recover the embassy compound for the United States. Unfortunately, it became clear within the next several hours that Bazargan and Yazdi had lost their influence in the internal struggles of the revolution, and they were dismissed. Within the next several hours also it became clear that the Ayatollah Khomeini was lending his support to the militants that were occupying the U.S. embassy compound.

President Carter, seeking to establish direct communication with the Iranian government, dispatched Ramsey Clark, a former attorney general, who had in the past been critical of the Shah's government. After some discussion the Iranian authorities refused to receive Clark, and the chances of establishing a new link with Iran faded.

Recognizing that the holding of hostages was a serious breach of diplomatic practice that could have repercussions for all embassies, other countries quickly rallied to support the demand of the United States that the hostages be released and that the embassy compound be returned to the United States. The action was supported in the United Nations Security Council and in representations by friendly governments to the authorities in Tehran. None of the appeals was effective. It became increasingly clear that the United States and Iran were facing a protracted crisis.

The crisis was not to end until January of 1981. Through the intervening months it was to pass through five distinct phases. In each of these phases Ambassador Probst and his Swiss colleagues played indispensable roles.

The period from November 4 until mid-December 1979 was marked by the opening of various diplomatic efforts and by the release of thirteen of the hostages. A second period, which lasted roughly from mid-December until mid-January 1980, was marked by an increase of international pressures and a move toward economic sanctions against Iran. The third period, from January through April, saw various efforts—by the secretary-general of the United Nations, by the UN Security Council working through an international commission, and by individual intermediaries—to develop a process for the release of the hostages.

These efforts were not successful, and in April the United States moved to apply greater pressure on Iran. This was partly sparked by the lack of success in the various diplomatic efforts and by indications as early as March that Khomeini had decreed that the hostages would remain in the hands of the militants until their fate was decided by the Iranian Parliament.

Parallel with the various developments in the hostage question, the implementation of Khomeini's Islamic constitution had been proceeding. Some had predicted, from the beginning, that Khomeini would not release the hostages until political institutions of his own making had been created. This process had begun in December 1979 with a referendum on the constitution. The Parliament was not elected until the latter part of May and did not convene for its first sitting until May 28.

Facing, therefore, the apparent decision of the Ayatollah and the slow process in the creation of new governmental institutions, the United States took steps in April to demonstrate its determination to move Iran toward release of the hostages. On April 7, diplomatic relations with Iran were broken and a formal embargo on U.S. exports was imposed. Restrictions were placed on the use of U.S. passports for travel to Iran. And, finally, a military rescue mission was attempted, unsuccessfully.

During the summer of 1980 the new political institutions of the Iranian revolution, and particularly the Parliament, began to function. International pressures on Iran for the release of the hostages continued. On July 10 one of the hostages, Richard Queen, was released because of illness. On July 27 the exiled Shah died in Cairo. While he had been central to the issue of the militants at the beginning, his death did not fundamentally change the situation. Khomeini remained resolved to use the holding of the hostages for maximum political benefits.

Economic sanctions against Iran, although they had not been formally approved by the Security Council because of a Soviet veto, were placed in effect by most nations friendly to the United States. Diplomatic representations on behalf of the United States by friendly nations continued.

Finally, in late August the United States received word through Germany of the readiness of an Iranian representative to meet secretly with an American representative. The Iranian representative was able to advise the United States in advance of conditions that Khomeini would publicly announce for the release of the hostages. It was clear that, for the first time, Khomeini himself was prepared to be identified with conditions for the release of the hostages.

This contact and the subsequent action of the Iranian Parliament opened the way for the final negotiations that led to the release of the hostages in January 1981. Algeria, which had previously been asked by Iran to represent that country to the United States, served as the intermediary in protracted negotiations.

The Swiss government first entered the scene in November of 1979 when, after negotiations involving the Palestine Liberation Organization, the Iranians agreed to release thirteen of the hostages, women and blacks. The Swiss government, aware of this, volunteered an offer to use a Swiss civilian aircraft to bring the thirteen out of Iran. While the Iranians would not agree to a special aircraft, the Swiss, through Ambassador Probst, kept us constantly advised of what was transpiring and helped us find out how the former hostages were leaving Iran. This first offer demonstrated the understanding on the part of the Swiss of the concern that this issue presented to the United States. It also demonstrated the capacity of neutral Switzerland to be helpful in the revolutionary atmosphere in Iran.

Even without that offer, it would have been natural for the United States to turn to Switzerland when a third country was needed to assist the United States or to represent the United States in the event of a break in diplomatic negotiations. Switzerland was already representing U.S. interests in another difficult country, Cuba. Swiss activity on behalf of the United States during 1980 included not only the efforts made on behalf of a resolution of the hostage crisis, but also interventions with the Government of Cuba when some 275 Cubans took refuge in the U.S. interests section of the Swiss embassy in Havana. Ambassador Probst was involved in these problems at the same time he was helping on Iran.

The Swiss reputation for professional, objective, and effective service on behalf of a nation in a troubled relationship had already been well established, but the Iranian hostage crisis was unusual in many ways. Despite the major crisis existing between the United States and Iran, neither nation at the outset of the situation wanted to break relations. As long as there was the faintest possibility that American Chargé Bruce Laingen might have some influence from his position of semi-captivity in the Foreign Ministry, the United States did not want to take a step that might further jeopardize his access. The Iranians found their embassy in the United States useful for propaganda on behalf of the revolution.

It was not until April that, in a period of maximum pressure, the United States formally broke diplomatic relations with Iran and asked Switzerland to assume the responsibilities of protecting power. Switzerland, which already had been involved and helpful to the United States since early in the crisis, was a natural choice for the role.

Late in November of 1979, the United States, fearful of a possible trial of the hostages and the possible execution of some, decided that a very clear message must be sent to Iran on the consequences of such actions. The sending of a message from the United States to Iran at that period was not an easy matter. It was unlikely that the Iranians would have accepted any message directly from an American, and a number of America's other friends were having their own problems in postrevolutionary Iran. Some had withdrawn their ambassadors, and others faced special bilateral problems that made them unwilling to intervene in a specific matter involving the United States. At a meeting in Secretary of State Cyrus Vance's office, the question of how best to transmit such a message was discussed. It was finally decided that the Swiss channel represented the best possibility.

I can recall making the request to a receptive Ambassador Probst. He promptly put the matter to the Foreign Department, which subsequently agreed. It was the first of many messages that were to be transmitted by the Swiss through the duration of this crisis.

For the Swiss, the crisis between the United States and Iran presented problems seldom found in other situations in which the Swiss had been asked to represent U.S. interests. Any action taken was likely to encounter the deep antagonism toward the United States expressed by the leaders of the Iranian revolution. No Iranian leader would receive an American or even messages from Americans which might compromise his own position in the revolution. To protect their political positions, Iranian officials receiving messages from the United States were likely very quickly to make them public.

The Iranian revolutionary leaders also made it clear that they were operating under a different set of understandings than those which govern normal diplomatic relationships. They could not, therefore, be counted on to follow the Vienna Convention which had governed practices within the international community for many years.

The holding of the hostages meant that the Swiss did not have access to U.S. diplomatic property, which was under the effective control of the captors. Efforts to deliver messages on behalf of the interests of the United States were further complicated by the lack of clear authority within postrevolutionary Iran. Throughout the year its various leaders were jockeying for access to Khomeini and for personal power. With the exception of a very few close to him, Khomeini kept most of the political rivals off balance. Regardless of the titles that a person might hold, it was therefore difficult for diplomats to determine his level of authority and whether the message passed to him would ever reach Khomeini himself. Finally, there was the peculiar circumstance that, throughout this period, the U.S. chargé d'affaires was present not only in the country, but in the Ministry of Foreign Affairs.

The diplomats of Switzerland performed three valuable tasks during this period. Throughout these many months they provided the principal channel of communication for the United States to Iran. There were other diplomatic friends prepared to deliver and transmit messages. There was also the strange fact that the teletype into the Iranian Foreign Ministry continued to work during most of the period, and it was possible for the U.S. State Department to send unclassified messages to Laingen himself. To those of us in the State Department at that time, however, no channel equaled in reliability that through Ambassador Probst and the Swiss Foreign Department to Ambassador Erik Lang in Tehran. Ambassador Lang often went to extraordinary efforts to assure that a message was delivered. On one occasion, for example, Lang waited for six hours in an antechamber before he could personally see President Bani-Sadr.

Communication involved more than the simple transmission of messages. At the Washington end, Ambassador Probst would telephone, either to me or to Assistant Secretary Harold Saunders, saying that he had a message. We would clear our calendar and be ready to sit with him as he read and translated the latest from Tehran, together with any interpretive comment that may have been added by Bern. At the other end, Ambassador Lang often attempted to convey, not only the text of the message, but the mood of Washington and, possibly, separate comments of his own Foreign Department.

Subjects ranged from the relatively routine to such critical messages as the possible U.S. response to the holding of trials.

The Swiss during this period were asked to assist in getting payment for Iranian employees of the American embassy, jobless after the hostage seizure. Ambassador Lang intervened to arrange for a doctor to visit the three Americans held in the Foreign Ministry. The Swiss pursued relentlessly the question of visits by clergymen and doctors to the hostages in the embassy. They pressed hard—and unsuccessfully until the end—for a complete list of the hostages. The Swiss diplomatic bag carried mail to Chargé Laingen and to the Swiss Foreign Department for the other hostages. One of the most difficult tasks effectively carried out by the Swiss was arranging for the return of the bodies of the eight U.S. military men killed in the abortive rescue attempt.

The second valuable service was that of providing assessments of the situation in Iran and descriptions of the atmosphere in Tehran. Cut off from its own embassy and with only the occasional reports from other friendly missions, the United States lacked the kind of on-the-spot description of conditions, personalities, and events that are essential in evaluating the nature of a problem and the prospects for solution. Ambassador Lang, by his own astute observation and his diligent inquiries, provided this kind of essential observation for the United States in a manner thoroughly appropriate for a representing power. His reporting was particularly useful during periods when there were visiting delegations, such as that of the secretary-general of the United Nations or the special commission set up by the secretary-general. Those delegations themselves, while cooperative in sharing assessments with U.S. representatives upon their return from Iran, were often not in the position to communicate while they were participating in the feverish programs established by the Iranian authorities. Ambassador Lang's reporting helped us to understand the conditions under which these missions were operating and the realistic limits of their accomplishments.

Finally, Ambassador Probst, with the full support and assistance of his foreign minister and his colleagues in Bern, was a valuable counselor to us in the State Department. The Swiss often had a different and valuable perspective on the possible alternatives open to the United States. The Swiss diplomats were alert to efforts to frustrate solutions and to complicate relations between the United States and Iran. It was Ambassador Lang in late March of 1980 who first alerted the United States to a false letter, purportedly from President Carter to Khomeini, circulating in Tehran at that time. The Swiss channel enabled the United States to send authentic letters to President Bani-Sadr very soon thereafter. On April 1, it was Ambassador Probst who telephoned the White House early in the morning to report Bani-Sadr's plan to transfer the hostages to government control. These plans were part of a significant agreed scenario frustrated at the last minute by Khomeini himself.

During February and March, two private individuals, Hector Villalon and Christian Bourguet, with access to those around Khomeini, played important roles in trying to find a formula to end the crisis. The Swiss diplomats were one of the principal channels of communication with Villalon and Bourguet when the two of them were in Iran. The Swiss arranged hospitality and sites for meetings between the two emissaries and U.S. representatives.

The Swiss role did not end with the opening of the final negotiation between the United States and Iran through Algeria. Swiss and Algerian representatives worked closely together. During the first meeting of Ambassador Probst with the Algerian ambassador to Washington, Redha Malek, to discuss the Iranian representation problem, the two men discovered that they had known each other during the French-Algerian talks at Evian in 1960. Ambassador Probst had been the Swiss representative to the Algerian delegation and Ambassador Malek the spokesman for the Algerian delegation.

In a February 1981 statement to the Congress on the Iranian hostage negotiations, Deputy Secretary of State Warren Christopher, speaking of the period of the Algerian role, said: "Throughout the negotiations, the Swiss represented our interests in Tehran with great vigor and great fidelity."[1] This statement could well have been made and applied to all of the phases of the hostage crisis.

Unassuming in claiming credit, professional in conduct and assessment, and totally reliable in objectivity and discretion, the Swiss, and Ambassador Probst in particular, could not be equalled in their cooperation and assistance to another country in need.

4

Evacuation and Hand-over to a Protecting Power
The Baghdad Embassy in 1967

Grant V. McClanahan

Grant McClanahan served in the U.S. Department of State as a career Foreign Service officer from 1946 to 1969. His overseas assignments included a tour of duty as chief political officer in the embassy in Baghdad in 1966–67. The following personal account of the events of five days in June 1967 illustrate both the human and administrative aspects of breaking diplomatic relations.

AT THE BEGINNING OF JUNE 1967, OUR FEELING IN THE American embassy in Baghdad, where I was chief of the political section, was that U.S.–Iraqi relations were fairly good and clearly improving. Then the abrupt outbreak of an Israeli-Arab war on June 5 led the Iraqis to sever relations with the United States on June 7, and with Britain on June 8. Iraq's notification of the severance required that all American nationals from the embassy depart on short notice. The American dependents and less essential personnel had already been evacuated overland, at midnight on June 6.

In the five-day period, June 5–9, there were some tense moments and awkward surprises. The experience illustrates how a hand-over to a protecting power can be effected, if necessary, under pressure of time—as well as what Foreign Service officers in Middle East capitals may need to have in the back of their minds when the telephone rings or they switch on the radio for a news broadcast.

The U.S. embassy in 1967 occupied a new and impressive property on the right bank of the Tigris River, adjacent to the presidential palace. The design by Louis Sert was handsome and efficient, with an ambassador's residence looking across the river, space for a tennis court and swimming pool, a garden with palm and fruit trees, staff quarters, and a well-planned chancery. The property had been acquired and planned when Iraq was governed by a friendly monarchy and seemed to be a promising country for U.S. commercial interests and a ready field for technical and military aid. It was, at the time, one of very few purpose-built U.S. embassies in the Middle East, and its design, like that of the modern consulate in Basra, symbolized America's postwar success and importance. The AID mission had withdrawn after the 1958 Iraqi military revolution. In the years since then, the embassy had come to have a well-staffed USIS, defense attachés of all the services (with the naval attaché resident in Tehran), an active cultural exchange program of U.S. professors in the universities, and a busy economic and commercial section.

There had been several indications that Iraq wished to upgrade relations. On January 30, 1967, the government named a new ambassador to Washington, Under Secretary for Foreign Affairs Nuri Jamil, to succeed Ambassador Nasir al Hani. Jamil, a senior military officer of the incumbent Arif regime, had been seconded to the Foreign Ministry for a time. He hoped to expand relations with Washington and, specifically, to recommend more exchanges of high-level visits.

Iraqi military and civilian attendance at the May 20 Armed Forces Day reception at our ambassador's residence had been exceptionally good. Even more significant, in mid-February 1967 an Iraqi military delegation had returned to Baghdad from a four-week visit to the United States under Major General Hasan Sabri and called their visit highly successful.

This atmosphere of normality and potential improvement prevailed when Ambassador Robert Strong left for home leave on April 13. There was not much concern about a possibly impending crisis and certainly none in U.S.–Iraqi relations. At the same time, we were conscious of the significant relationship between the Iraqi regime of President Abd al Rahman Arif and the regime of Gamal Abd al Nasser in Egypt. When the Iraqi regime had emerged in 1964 under Abd al Rahman's older brother, Abd al Salam Arif, an early move of the new leadership had been to visit Cairo.

At the beginning of June, there had been reports for several days of political tensions and military buildup by Egypt, Israel, and Syria, but I recall starting Monday morning in my third-floor office at the front of the chancery as usual. The day before, Sunday, I had attended a farewell brunch for my assistant, Thomas Scotes, who was leaving in a few days. That night at 10:25, FSO Peter Sutherland had arrived by Middle East Airlines from Beirut, carrying his Hans Wehr Arabic dictionary, to replace Tom Scotes. My appointments book records that there was to be an official dinner on Monday the 5th at 7:00 p.m. at Qasr al Abiadh for Nuri Jamil, the Iraqi ambassador-designate to Washington. It also notes that the event was canceled by telephone.

The Israeli attack on the Egyptian air force was launched across Sinai in the early daylight of Monday, June 5, but the full import of the news reached Baghdad slowly.

I glanced out my windows at the permanently manned anti-aircraft guns a few hundred yards away in the military park opposite the president's palace. The Iraqi gunners were slumped in their heavy jackets, bareheaded, occasionally yawning in the fresh morning air. I was alone and began writing the agenda for a Monday meeting I would chair about 9:30 a.m. which assigned items to be covered by the various embassy sections for a weekly summary despatch. One item was to be the safe arrival by air of a U.S. gift of sandbags to reinforce a crucial dike on the Euphrates. I had turned on the little radio beside my desk. The Iraqi Arabic news broadcast, as I recall it now, was quoting initial reports from European services that bombing had occurred and battles had commenced in Sinai.

I walked down the hall to consult the chargé, Enoch

Duncan. He was calm and serious and immediately thought of the embassy routines to be canceled and meetings to be postponed.

The news of heavy fighting in Sinai and the tone of the debates at the UN Security Council became increasingly ominous all through the 5th and 6th of June. Through the USIS news channels and other media sources we heard of the "big lie" about American and British armed assistance to Israel's campaign.[1] On June 5, "the Egyptian Armed Forces Supreme Command charged that American and British planes provided fighter cover over Israel during raids by Israeli aircraft," saying "it had 'actual proof' that American and British aircraft carriers played a role in the Israeli aggression."[2] This charge was categorically denied the next evening, June 6, at the Security Council by both the United States and the United Kingdom representatives, who invited a UN investigation.

Iraq's delegate on June 6 complained of U.S. unwillingness to call "for the withdrawal of forces back to positions held before the outbreak of hostilities." However, he did not mention either the charge in the "big lie" nor say that Iraq would sever relations with the United States.

The Syrian representative in the debate attacked the United States and the United Kingdom as "enemies of the Arab nation [who] acted in collusion with Israel by joining in the air attack against Arab towns and by providing air cover for the Israel armed forces." He announced the severing of diplomatic relations with the United States by Syria, along with Algeria, Iraq, and the United Arab Republic. In reply, the U.K. and U.S. representatives "reiterated their categorical denials of participation in the conflict."

On the afternoon of June 7 at the Security Council, the United Arab Republic delegate again charged "that the United States and the United Kingdom had participated in the air operations on Israel's side." The U.S. and U.K. representatives "again rejected the charges...and repeated their proposals for a United Nations investigation on the spot."[3]

A Crisis Atmosphere

A grimly funny incident illustrates unpleasant surprises in sudden emergencies such as that we then faced. The embassy property had been attacked by a mob, which came over the front wall on the morning of Tuesday, June 6. After a brief, spirited attack, the mob withdrew. That night the embassy staff reviewed tactics, in case it should happen again the following morning. Our defensive equipment included some tear gas in small, throwable canisters. When one of these was brought out to demonstrate their use, however, two drawbacks soon came to light. First, when the top was unscrewed to let out a short sample hiss of gas, it would not shut off again, and the demonstration canister had to be set outside to "waste its sweetness" on the night air instead of smelling up the embassy. The other drawback was that the printed instruction label on each canister stated plainly that it had been manufactured in Israel. Hardly the defensive device to toss into an aroused crowd of anti-U.S. demonstrators during that particular Middle East crisis! The decision was to lock up and seal that equipment away.

Not to overlook or shrink from the obvious, it is important to have and to expend carefully the accumulated fund of good personal relations at a time of crisis such as June 1967. Local friendships and even loyalties are put to the test. We were grateful that our ambassador, though absent, was well known and personally respected by then Iraqi President and Prime Minister Abd al Rahman Arif. Though we had almost no contacts during the crisis with senior personalities (Foreign Minister Adnan Pachachi was in New York at the United Nations), several of the working-level officials found reasons to stop by the embassy and make discreet reassurances.

The American staff in Baghdad resided in widely separated individual houses. I think their good relations with their immediate neighbors helped explain why there were no incidents or threats to people or property. My own house and garden on the Tigris had the Bulgarian ambassador immediately contiguous downstream and the U.A.R. ambassador's residence immediately upstream. I had comfortable personal contact with both. Telephone conversations with Iraqi friends, though guarded in tone, were possible and sometimes heartening. Such personal evidence of real feelings was a helpful antidote to the buffeting output of television, radio, and press, which had the rhetorical intensity of a desert sandstorm.

The round-the-clock police guard at the embassy chancery, placed there after a demonstration, was stolidly dutiful. The guards were appreciative of the food and water the embassy provided them and personally agreeable to officers who came and went at all hours through the gates.

Late one night the chargé had to go alone with a driver to the Foreign Ministry on a matter of American concern. The ministry was dark and the sentries outside the gate apparently had no key to open the gate for the car to pass through. One sentry obligingly climbed over the ministry's spiked gate and went into the building to locate a key. It turned out there were a few officials on duty, and the chargé was able to transact his urgent business with them.

One Iraqi Foreign Ministry official who came to pay a brief farewell call on the chargé and me remarked over coffee that the decision to sever relations was now a fact. Whatever our views, the only thing was to make its implementation as smooth as possible.

In normal times every well-managed embassy section has a natural level of busy activity. In the special situation of June 1967 some functional differences appeared. The chargé's office and the political section became more commanding and less coordinating. This is natural at such times, for suddenly everyone wants to know the significance of the latest information and to hear the latest decisions. The focus therefore narrows to the person in charge (the ambassador, if present, or the chargé) and to the political section, as the best available sources. That week in Baghdad, even the daily local press summary, normally provided by USIS, was regularly produced under the political section by local employees.

The economic section has a relative pause in its activities, except perhaps to maintain contact with local American business persons. In Baghdad, for example, the head of the economic section was put in charge of supervising the ambassador's vacant residence and the priority program of packing the ambassador's effects for shipment to America.

The defense attachés' offices become even more self-contained than usual in an emergency. They have their own security and logistical procedures. In Baghdad, the military attachés' offices took care of themselves effectively and were able to assist others. For example, the senior defense attaché, Army Colonel Neil Robinson, was put in charge of organizing the final motor convoy and handled all its details well.

The Marine guard in Baghdad, about ten men, with quarters on the embassy compound, worked hard and enthusiastically, collecting and destroying classified papers and maintaining intensified internal security quietly and inconspicuously. These Marines moved out with the final convoy.

The administrative section had greatly stepped-up responsibilities. In an atmosphere of urgency they needed simultaneously to look after the U.S. government's property and prepare it for a tidy hand-over, to designate local employees who would provide technical help to the protecting power, and to push through arrangements for shipping the American staffs' personal effects.

In the Baghdad situation, this last task was complicated by the fact that on June 8 the Iraqi government had abruptly severed relations with Britain, and therefore all the British embassy personnel also needed to have their effects packed and shipped. It was a boom time of opportunity for the rather small packing and shipping companies of Baghdad! Under the stress of the times there were soon shortages of wrapping paper and padding, not to mention skilled packers. At our embassy, an excellent senior local employee, Jessie Jureidini, followed through after we left. In time, our effects arrived at their destination with very few losses and breakages.

From the first day almost to the final departures at the end of the fifth, there was a continual stream of urgent, necessary actions. These would make too long a list, but it may be useful to mention a few. Each office put classified papers into large paper bags, which were put in the halls, collected by the Marines, and burnt outdoors in cylindrical rotating wire incinerators. Uncoded, basic material was placed in the combination-locked file drawers. They were then wheeled into strong rooms to be sealed behind doors just before our departure.

At home at night, people packed their valuables and necessities to take in the convoy. Servants had to be reassured and paid off. I gave my television set to our Assyrian house servant and my American manual lawn mower to the Shiite Arab gardener. Pets had to be settled into baskets and cages for evacuation or given to the best possible homes. All the cars and trucks for the convoy were given full tanks of gasoline from the embassy's supply in the compound.

The embassy's commissary had canned goods and packaged goods and many American convenience items, all, of course, imported through customs duty-free and paid for with U.S. government funds. The administrative section called their opposite numbers in friendly embassies and arranged a few hours when diplomats and their wives could come with shopping baskets and freezer bags. They were entitled to diplomatic immunity from customs and were pleased to pay the marked prices, so the Iraqi and U.S. governments could have no reasonable financial complaints.

The Iraqi security authorities asked to have all diplomatic identity cards, driver's licenses, and passes of embassy personnel returned, and the administrative section so notified all individuals. We sent the cards to the office of the chief of section, the able, resourceful M. A. (Sandy) Sanderson, who sorted and bundled them by categories. A characteristically shrewd idea of his was to deface or rip off each identification photo from the documents we were returning. He remarked that the Americans had supplied the photos, and why should we voluntarily make the files of the security authorities more complete?

Evacuation

The intensifying military situation and menacing UN debate
had led to our early decision to evacuate embassy dependents
and nonessential personnel. They would depart at midnight on
Tuesday, June 6.

There was a normal bus transport service to carry Iranian
Shiite pilgrims from Iranian cities across Iraq to the Shiite holy
cities of Kerbela and Nejaf in Southwest Iraq. The vehicles
were Iranian-owned, and the drivers were Iranians. When the
embassy decided to move the dependents, the administrative
section quietly located Iranian buses and their drivers and
contracted to have them carry our passengers from the dike
road along the Tigris, just upstream from our embassy, to the
U.S. embassy in Tehran, which in 1967 was as safe a haven as
an American citizen could find in the Middle East.

The word was passed among the embassy families that
afternoon. The passengers could each take a suitcase. It was
hoped they would only be going temporarily, and that even if
all had to depart now, some would be returning soon to a U.S.
interests section to be established under the flag of a protecting
power's embassy.

The convoy consisted of about three or four buses, each
holding about thirty passengers. There were also about twenty
private cars. So many women and children needed a few
American men to accompany them. The cultural exchange
professors and others were also going. FSO Peter Sutherland,
who, it will be recalled, had only arrived in Baghdad late on
the evening before the war broke out, was put in charge of the
group and thus departed Tuesday after arriving Saturday. He
was an Arabist and unaccompanied, and he accepted the
assignment loyally.

My wife, who was on one of the buses that night, was in
charge of keeping custody of all the passports, helping ex-
hausted mothers with sick children, and, most crucial of
responsibilities, standing behind the Iranian bus driver and
talking with him to insure that he neither went to sleep at the
wheel (he had driven the hundreds of miles from Iran only a

couple of hours earlier) nor got into a dangerous race with the other bus drivers on the curving road through the Iranian Zagros mountains in the hours before dawn.

Time was in short supply that week in June. Night action messages were flying about between Washington and the Middle East posts.[4] Not many were repeated to Baghdad, even from such key areas as Cairo, Tel Aviv, Amman, and the U.S. delegation at the United Nations. Our capital may have seemed peripheral to Washington, and our ambassador was not there to weigh in from his post. Perhaps we did not deserve more than second-level priority.

On the afternoon of Wednesday, June 7, the chargé and I called by invitation at the Foreign Ministry. We were received by a middle-ranking official (the supervisor of the economic department, as I recall) in whose comfortable office we were served coffee. He informed us Iraq was formally breaking relations with the United States in the wake of U.S. armed forces having assisted the Israeli forces in their attack on Arab countries. The chargé broke in to repeat that he was officially authorized to deny this allegation. (As noted, the U.S. and U.K. representatives at the Security Council on the previous evening had categorically denied any participation of their aircraft in the hostilities.) The Foreign Ministry official politely but firmly terminated discussion of that point by saying that Iraq had been told the facts by its Syrian ally, whose word it accepted. He gave us a rather faint ozalid copy of a two-page, typed Arabic document. This laid out Iraqi terms for our withdrawal, which was to include all Americans at the embassy. The head of mission had three days and the other Americans at the embassy a longer time, about a week, as I remember.

On our ride back from the Foreign Ministry, the chargé told me that *all* embassy personnel would depart within the short, three-day period of the Iraqi deadline for the chargé. He emphasized that in such a volatile situation, full diplomatic immunity was a priceless asset which could be most effectively asserted by an ambassador or his deputy.

The whole interview had not lasted more than fifteen minutes. It was polite but perfunctory, rather as though the official had been given little notice and no background on his démarche. Yet those few minutes and that unimpressive little document were enough official action to sever diplomatic relations. Seventeen years, a drastic change of regime in Iraq, and five American presidential administrations would pass before diplomatic relations were to be formally restored.

The Protecting Power. With the break in relations on June 7, the question of choosing a country to represent the United States in Iraq immediately arose. Initially during the crisis in Iraqi-United States relations, the State Department apparently anticipated that Turkey would be a good candidate for the role of protecting power for U.S. interests in Iraq, but the U.S. embassy in Ankara soon found that the government there was cool toward the idea.[5]

Turkey may have considered its relations with neighboring Iraq in 1967 to be so important, due to such matters as trade, the Kirkuk oil fields, future pipelines, and the shared Kurdish question, that it did not want to be encumbered by the burden of responsibilities for the United States in Iraq at a time when American policies in the Arab countries were receiving much local criticism and official denunciations. The Turkish embassy in Baghdad was behaving toward the U.S. embassy in an aloof, circumspect manner. One of their middle-level diplomats told us that in case of necessity they might be able to handle some routine consular services for us at their embassy, such as notarizing a document or transmitting a commercial inquiry, but beyond that he could not be sure. Ultimately, Belgium was approached, and the government in Brussels readily accepted.

The ambassador of Belgium in Baghdad was Marcel Dupret. A neat, energetic man, he had been at the post at least two years. He was well-liked and had been a pleasant companion on an overnight expedition a group of us organized to the ruined early Parthian city of Hatra in northern Iraq. He was in touch with us early in the crisis, having reported to Brussels that the question of a protecting power for U.S. interests had not been settled, that it was a troubling problem, and that if there was urgent need, he thought Belgium should be prepared to assist.

When the Turkish possibility persisted in its uncertainty, our chargé invited Dupret to call. He came promptly. A vivid memory among all the rush of events was the moment when I met him at our chancery's entrance. When he entered the ambassador's office where the chargé was now working, the chargé came forward to greet him and clasped Dupret's hand warmly in both of his. Enoch Duncan was not a demonstrative personality, but his pleasure, relief, and satisfaction were obvious. Dupret was instantly reassuring and made an offer of any assistance within his power. Duncan told him our situation candidly, and everything was settled in principle in a few minutes.

Dupret told us part of the explanation for his forthcoming attitude. At the end of World War II, he had been in a part of Belgium liberated by American forces. For some days there had been rumors that the Americans were coming. As he recalled: "When I first saw the American soldiers in battle dress coming in the distance and then into our street, I thought, this is the happiest moment of my life. If ever in the future I have an opportunity to do something helpful for the United States at a moment of need, I'll remember this time and try to show my gratitude." Nothing could have been better for our morale than to hear this from him.

Ambassador Dupret readily agreed to tell the Iraqi Foreign Ministry of Belgium's willingness to be the protecting power and to follow up with them on any messages we might need to convey. With Foreign Minister Pachachi in New York at the United Nations, Dupret's entrée as an ambassador could be a valuable asset to have among the officials acting for their foreign minister.

At the meeting with Dupret, we agreed that as soon as we Americans left it would be a positive symbolic action for him personally to spend the night in our ambassador's residence. Probably this precaution against an unexpected or informal intrusion was not necessary. However, the residence was an extremely desirable property and the whole compound, as noted earlier, was temptingly convenient to the presidential palace.[6]

Preparations. On the morning of Thursday, June 8, we held a meeting at the chancery for Americans resident in Baghdad. The consular section was in charge of telephoning the invitations and asking those who were reached to pass the word to any who could not be contacted. Telephone service in Baghdad, as I recall, worked normally, that is, fairly well, during the crisis week.

There were not many American businessmen and other nonofficial persons in Baghdad that summer, and very few of them had dependents still there. The meeting therefore consisted of only about twenty or thirty persons, many of them already acquainted with one another. The Iraqi government had provided the embassy with a police guard at the gate, and an embassy officer, probably of the administrative section, was at the gate to identify these appropriate visitors (and to see them out after the meeting).

Chargé Duncan counseled everyone to keep a low profile and stay indoors. He told them the official embassy staff would all be departing late the following evening. There would be a motor convoy, mostly of our own private cars, and space in the cars for passengers with one or two medium-sized suitcases. He offered an opportunity for raising questions and for discussion, but there was not much of either. Most unofficial people had been able to follow the situation on the BBC World Service and, to a lesser extent, the Voice of America.

On the last afternoon, June 9, I went with Ambassador Dupret and Sanderson, our administrative chief, to seal the doors of storage rooms with sealing wax. It is not easy to apply a heated, soft glob of sealing wax to the vertical crack between a door and its jamb, but somehow we managed, with a guttering candle and a strong flashlight to use in dark corridors.

Damage to the embassy façade by the street mob that momentarily came over the wall on the second day had to be surveyed, reported, and put into form for a later claim. Fortunately, the alluvial nature of Iraq's geologic structure makes stones fairly hard for a mob to come by. However, the available broken bricks and lesser missiles had shattered a few of our windows. In such an environment, one had to be stoical.

Departure. By about midafternoon on Friday, June 9, all
actions judged to be essential had been taken and reported. I
believe that Enoch Duncan spent his final hours in the ambassador's office completing a general think-piece cable. He sent
me to his house some distance from the chancery to give final
instructions to his two house servants and to report on the
situation there. As we went through the streets, newsboys were
hawking Baghdad Arabic newspapers with six-inch headlines
saying "No!" This word expressed the rejection of Nasser's
broadcast offer to resign and accept responsibility for the
military defeat. I had listened to the text of Nasser's speech
being read in deliberate, lugubrious tones by an Iraqi announ-
cer on Baghdad radio, and we had listened at the embassy to
the crowds of students and others rushing along Abu Nawwas
Street on the opposite bank of the Tigris shouting rhythmical-
ly, *"La, ya Gamal!"* ("No, O Gamal!").

When the time came, the chargé made his departure
through the front entrance, from which our official U.S. shield
had been lowered and stored away a few hours earlier. His car,
with a Marine driver in civilian clothes, was ready. Several of
us shook his hand, and the head of the Iraqi police guard
saluted him. He smiled and exchanged a few words in Arabic.
Then the car pulled out of the gate, with a police escort leading
the way out of Baghdad. It was a businesslike but far from
cheerful moment.

The convoy formed up that evening under a dark sky with
a thin crescent moon. I had spent my few hours as chargé
mainly in a walking tour for a last survey of the vacant offices
and grounds. After dark, I moved into the ambassador's office
and conferred briefly with section heads. I appropriated three
symbolic souvenirs: a cylindrical scrap of hardened aluminum,
which had been left behind on the floor of the empty code
room when the machines were crated and removed, a plastic
thermos pitcher from the ambassador's desk, and one of the
embassy library's better Arabic-English dictionaries, just before
that room's books were sealed up. The code room brought me
the forms for the final sign-off cable. I put down a few observations, concluding with the Arabic farewell phrase *"fi iman*

Allah" ("in the keeping of God"), and typed my name. The code room asked what the last words meant and I explained. Months later in the State Department, several people mentioned they had seen the final cable from the Baghdad embassy and thought the words were a garble!

Duncan had been confident the city streets would be dark and deserted, and thus secure for our convoy, by about 11:00 p.m. The convoy left the gates of the compound at 10:30. His judgment was absolutely correct.

The route ran via Baquba to cross the frontier just beyond Khanaqin. In the early light of Saturday the 10th, we passed through Iranian controls at their big customs shed at Qasr-e-Shirin. On we drove, then, through Kermanshah and onto the new road through the Zagros. I and others fell asleep a few times at the wheel, but were saved by a shout from our businessmen passengers. At Hamadan, we met the chargé, who looked relieved, and we all rested on the cots and bunks of the hospitable U.S. military mission post. It seemed an easy drive the next day to the gates of the Tehran embassy.

The Aftermath

We were fortunate to have the strongly manned Tehran embassy as our group's destination. We were the beneficiaries of Tehran's established routine for receiving Middle East embassy evacuees. On arriving at the spacious garden compound, for example, our weary dependents found a row of cheerful little striped tents set up and manned by Tehran embassy wives. At one, money could be changed; at others, one learned of hotel assignments, babysitting arrangements, health information, and the like. The Tehran embassy's facilities were far more extensive than those we had had in Baghdad, and we welcomed the hospitality and helpfulness of their staff. We were about 250 persons altogether, but they coped with our immediate needs most effectively.

Even when the hand-over to a protecting power takes place on short notice and against a background of uncooperative or unpredictable host government attitudes, planning for an immediate or future U.S. interests section with an American staff needs to be done. My impression is that Washington tends to be optimistic in such situations and is much more prepared to hear of positive developments than to accept a gloomy prediction. In 1967 in Iraq, I believe, the Department of State did not anticipate a resumption of early and full relations. Its action in reassigning Chargé Duncan to be DCM in Amman a few days after his arrival in Tehran indicated that they thought he would not be needed to head up Baghdad.

In my relations with the U.S. embassy in Tehran, I was careful to behave neither as "an embassy in exile" nor as a destitute relative at a family reunion. Our situation was, realistically speaking, that of a group of Foreign Service families awaiting new assignment and transfer. The transfer of a very few might possibly turn out to be back to Baghdad, but that never seemed likely, and I anticipated that after a few months, the State Department would be ready to use the final curtain line of I Pagliacci, "*La commedia è finita.*"

In the period of June through September 1967, when I was kept at the embassy in Tehran in readiness to head a hoped-for American interests section under the flag of the Belgian embassy in Baghdad, my official contacts were drastically changed from what they had been as chief of the Baghdad political section. They were confined to my host, the U.S. embassy in Tehran, and my possible future host, the Belgian embassy in Baghdad.

With the embassy in Tehran, we "refugees" from Baghdad tried to be as little of a burden for as short a time as possible. The embassy gave us a large room on the ground floor of their chancery near the main entrance. There, with desks and a telephone, administrative officer Sandy Sanderson worked, and former Baghdad personnel could come to leave messages and ask for advice or assistance. I worked in a room near Political Counselor Martin Herz, and for the first couple of weeks my wife and I were house guests of the Herzes until we found a hotel room and later an apartment. Other Americans from Baghdad lived in hotels. As they were reassigned, most flew direct from Tehran to Washington. Several of them wrote personal letters to me from Washington, occasionally offering crumbs of information on what they had learned of the outlook for the intended interests section.

I proposed to Chargé Nicholas Thacher that he allow a time once a week when I could come with Sanderson to his office and report on our situation. He readily accepted, and our meetings with him usually lasted half an hour. Later we met with Ambassador Armin Meyer after he returned from home leave toward the end of summer.

With the Belgian embassy in Baghdad I had less contact, for there was no convenient means. The Belgian Foreign Ministry sent to Baghdad to handle U.S. interests a young diplomat, Counselor of Embassy Viscount Vilain, who spoke excellent English and had such a deep-rooted aristocratic family background that his full name ended with the Roman numerals "XXIIII." (This was thought by the code room to be a garble or an abbreviation the first time it appeared in a cable from Brussels.) He was efficient and practical. His expenses were paid by the U.S. government.

After about six weeks, he arranged to visit me in Tehran for a lengthy business luncheon. Afterwards, I reported his observations to Washington, most notably—and, as it turned out, accurately—that he did not expect the Iraqis to accept Americans in an interests section in the foreseeable future.

Part II

The Interests Section

The Interests Section

T HE DISCUSSION OF THE ROLE OF THE SWISS GOVERN-
ment on behalf of the United States in Iran illustrates
the traditional pattern of the protecting power. A new
form of relations among nations, the creation of "interests
sections," has developed since the end of World War II—in the
case of the United States in the aftermath of the 1967 Arab-
Israeli war. In effect, such sections are embassies, staffed by
each affected nation's own officers, operating under a foreign
flag. The next four chapters relate the experiences of three
U.S. diplomats who headed such sections in Algeria, Iraq,
Egypt, and Cuba, and of the Egyptian diplomat who headed
his country's interests section in Washington.

The interests section became a means of continuing virtually
full relations between countries while avoiding the political
symbolism that became attached to a resumption of relations.
The three Arab nations, along with two others, had broken
relations with the United States under the pressure of an Arab
League decision at a conference in Khartoum following the
outbreak of the 1967 war. The Arab move was based on a
widely believed, but false, allegation that the United States had
assisted Israel by providing air cover when Israeli planes
attacked Cairo.

The nations concerned were reluctant to resume relations
with the United States without a broader Arab consensus, but
Algeria and Egypt, in particular, felt the need to maintain
relations as near to normal as political circumstances permitted. The maintenance of U.S. personnel under a foreign flag
was easier in these two countries because American diplomats
had not been completely expelled, as they were in Iraq.

The Cuban case, as Mr. Smith's essay shows, was somewhat different. Relations had long been suspended between the United States and Cuba when the Carter administration came into office in 1977. An effort was made to move relations with Cuba back to a more normal basis. In this case, a full resumption of diplomatic relations would have been symbolically difficult for the United States. The interests section was agreed upon as a further, but interim, step.

5

U.S. Diplomacy under the Flag of Spain
Cairo, 1967–1974

Donald C. Bergus

Donald C. Bergus, retired Foreign Service officer and former ambassador, was counselor of the U.S. embassy in Cairo in 1962–65 and head of the U.S. interests section in Cairo from 1967 to 1971, under the Spanish flag.

ON JUNE 5, 1967, ISRAELI FORCES ATTACKED THE ARMED forces of Egypt on land, sea, and air. Within a few hours the Egyptian air force was destroyed. The humiliation of Egypt's army was soon to follow. Before the "Six-Day War" was halted by a UN-imposed cease-fire on June 10, Syrian and Jordanian forces had joined in the hostilities and had suffered equally devastating setbacks.

The cease-fire found Israeli forces occupying the whole of the Sinai Peninsula up to the east bank of the Suez Canal, all of Jordanian territory west of the River Jordan, and the strategic Golan Heights of Syria. What had started in mid-May as an unexpected challenge by Egypt's President Nasser to the United Nations arrangements, which had kept an uneasy but effective peace along Egypt's borders with Israel since the Suez War of 1956, ended in military disaster.

On the second day of the 1967 war, the Egyptian government, citing King Hussein of Jordan as its source of information, claimed that a major reason for Israel's air victory had been the active participation in the battle of American war planes operating from U.S. aircraft carriers in the Eastern Mediterranean. On the basis of this allegation (which was false), Egypt severed diplomatic relations with the United States. The American embassy in Cairo was informed that the entire American community in Egypt, official and nonofficial, must, with a few exceptions, leave the country. On June 10, this evacuation was accomplished with great difficulty and considerable hardship to the Americans involved.

In those last few days, arrangements were made for the protection of Egyptian interests in the United States by India and the protection of U. S. interests in Egypt by Spain. The selection of Spain as the protecting power in Egypt came as a surprise to many. The idea of asking Spain to take this responsibility first came from the American embassy in Cairo and had been endorsed almost automatically by the Department of State and the White House—despite the qualms of some at the prospect of having American interests represented by a Spain where General Franco was still very much in power and which had never established diplomatic relations with Israel.

As Egyptian-American relations began to worsen early in 1967, the American embassy in Cairo, in its contingency planning, had good reason to recommend Spain to look after its interests. The traditional candidate for such a position, Switzerland, was deeply involved in a number of thorny disputed cases arising from Egyptian nationalization or sequestration of properties owned by Swiss nationals of Egyptian origin. One of these cases had to do with the official residence of the American ambassador in Cairo, a situation which put the United States into an adversary position against the Swiss. Other possible protectors among our traditional friends were not available. Canada had been looking after British interests since Egypt severed relations with Britain over the Rhodesian question in the mid-1960s. Similarly, Italy was protecting the interests of the Federal Republic of Germany, which had incurred Egypt's wrath by establishing diplomatic relations with Israel in 1965.

Whatever the reasons, the choice of Spain to look after us proved to be an excellent one. A primary factor was the personality, background, and outlook of the Spanish ambassador to Egypt, His Excellency Angel Sagaz y Zubelzu. Ambassador Sagaz had seen extensive service in the United States before his assignment to Egypt. He was thus familiar with our ways, shared our pragmatism, and naturally evoked the respect and support of the Americans he worked with. He never found it necessary to insist on the niceties of protocol. His open, "let's-get-the-job-done" attitude made possible the expeditious establishment of working relationships between American representatives and Egyptian officials in Cairo, despite the mutual bitterness engendered by the circumstances that led to the breaking of relations. Ambassador Sagaz played this key role in Cairo until the spring of 1972, at which time he was, appropriately enough, transferred to Washington as ambassador of Spain to the United States. His distinguished service at that post was cut short only two years later by his tragic and unexpected death from cancer. His eminence as a practitioner of diplomacy was matched only by his integrity and compassion as a great human being.

One could cite many examples of Ambassador Sagaz's perspicacity and humanity. Two come to mind. In the hasty departure of June 1967, the American air attaché had left behind his official aircraft, the military equivalent of a Convair. The Egyptian authorities refused our several requests that a U.S. Air Force team be admitted to Egypt to evacuate the aircraft. The Spanish ambassador, noting that Iberian Airways flew Convairs on many of their routes, proposed that a Spanish civilian crew come to Egypt to fly the aircraft out of the country. There was some hesitation on the part of the Egyptian military, but after gentle and persistent prodding by Ambassador Sagaz, the operation was accomplished.

Much more important, however, was the role the Spanish ambassador played in the case of the Jewish community in Egypt. This had been a proud and numerous group whose roots in Egypt went back to the Hellenistic period. It will be recalled that the first translation of the Hebrew Bible into

Greek, the Septuagint, was accomplished in the third century B.C. to accommodate the Jewish community of Alexandria.

Egypt's Jewish community had long been dwindling, particularly since the Suez War of 1956. By 1967 only about two thousand remained. At the outbreak of the June War, all male Jews of military age were imprisoned by the Egyptians. The Spanish ambassador took the lead in extending protection to the Jewish women, children, and older men who had not been imprisoned. He worked unceasingly for the release of the prisoners. He invoked Spanish laws which gave him the right to grant Spanish passports to Egyptian Jews on the basis that their ancestors might have resided in Spain prior to the Spanish Inquisition. By the summer of 1970, the prisoners had been released and the entire Jewish community safely evacuated. For this act he earned the recognition and gratitude of us all. The American Joint Distribution Committee, on its own initiative, made a substantial contribution to CARITAS, Madame Sagaz's favorite charity in Egypt, as a sign of its appreciation.

The United States made a formal request in Madrid on or about June 7, 1967, that Spain assume the role of protecting power. According to Ambassador Sagaz, the request was referred directly to General Franco. The Spanish head of state quickly assented. He also directed that, contrary to normal diplomatic practice in these situations, the Spanish government would bear any costs arising from the assumption of this role and that no bills for expenses should be sent to the United States. In mid-June, Madrid sent two career Spanish diplomats of the rank of first secretary to Cairo to assist the Americans. Their salaries and allowances were borne directly by the Spanish government. As the operations of the United States interests section of the Embassy of Spain took shape and developed into a workable pattern, these two officers had less and less to do and Ambassador Sagaz returned them to Spain by the end of August 1967.

Again, contrary to usual diplomatic practice, there was never any written agreement between Spain and the United States covering the details of the relationship. Things were worked out on the spot in response to specific problems and needs. There never arose a reason for referring a matter to Madrid or Washington for guidance or resolution.

At the time of the June 10 evacuation of the bulk of the American official and nonofficial community from Egypt, the Egyptians indicated that five members of the embassy staff could remain behind to form the nucleus of a United States interests section. The senior embassy officer whom the Egyptians had expected to remain to head the section declined to do so. Another senior embassy officer volunteered to remain but was declared unacceptable by the Egyptians. The task of temporarily heading the section devolved upon William B. Bromell, a first secretary from the embassy political section. Staying on with him were Martin Armstrong, administrative officer; Richard Weitzel, fiscal officer; and Lee Graham and Roger Hyde, communications personnel.

To this group fell the overwhelming task of liquidating a diplomatic establishment that had been the largest American embassy in the Middle East, with all the usual ancillary organizations: a large AID mission; a defense attaché establishment, with three military attachés, other military personnel, and two aircraft; regional attaché offices; an active U.S. Information Service program, including an American Library and widely popular English language classes; a U.S. Naval Medical Research unit; and even a branch of the Library of Congress.

Dismantling all this involved packing and shipping back to the United States the furniture, automobiles, and personal goods of nearly two hundred families who had been evacuated. This task could not have been accomplished without the close and careful supervision of senior Egyptian employees of the suddenly-former American embassy, most of whom had served the U.S. government faithfully for several decades.

A related and equally gargantuan task was the shutting down and mothballing of the extensive offices housing embassy and related operations. In its heyday the embassy occupied a number of former mansions covering most of a city block at the edge of the Cairo business district. This collection of buildings,

interspersed with lawns and gardens, had a pleasant atmosphere something like a university campus. In one corner of
this compound, a multistory former hotel had been acquired
by the embassy and converted to offices and some staff living
quarters. This structure became the nucleus of the interests
section. The rest of the buildings were closed and sealed. Over
what had been the flagship building of the embassy, the former
ambassador's office, now locked and shuttered, flew the flag
of Spain.

By the autumn of 1967, these administrative tasks had been
largely accomplished. The Embassy of Spain played an
invaluable role in this process. It gave the U.S. interests section
free use of its official seal, which served to expedite the
plethora of required documents so relished by the Egyptian
bureaucracy. Placards were printed with the following text in
English, Arabic, and Spanish against the background of the
Spanish flag: "This property under the protection of the
Embassy of Spain in the United Arab Republic." These were
placed on all American official properties in Cairo and Alexandria, even on the cars retained for the official use of the
interests section. They were never challenged.

Simultaneously, the Spanish ambassador conducted negotiations in Cairo looking toward the establishment of a written
basis for the existence and operations of the U.S. interests
section. An exchange of notes between the Embassy of Spain
and the Egyptian Foreign Ministry was accomplished on June
24, 1967. This exchange became known as the "Spanish
Protocol" (see text in annex to this chapter, pp. 76–78). It laid
down the ground rules for our operations in Egypt. It also, by
the principle of reciprocity, covered the operations of the
Egyptian interests section of the Embassy of India in
Washington.

The "Spanish Protocol" was relatively brief and quite simple.
It provided for the assignment to Cairo of an officer in charge,
three other American diplomats, and ten support personnel.
Each of these was to obtain the *agrément* of the Egyptian
government before assignment. In ordinary diplomatic
practice, of course, *agrément* is required only for the chief of

mission. Moreover, granting of full diplomatic status to only four individuals reflected the deep suspicions of the Egyptians in the wake of their military disaster. In practice, *agrément* was never refused. Moreover, the number of assigned personnel in each of the Cairo and Washington interests sections grew to sixteen by 1970.

This gradual expansion occurred entirely as the result of Egyptian initiatives. It was they who sought to increase their Washington staff from time to time and we were happy to reciprocate. Likewise, it was the Egyptians who proposed in the autumn of 1967 that the interests sections be headed by diplomats with the personal rank of minister plenipotentiary. Again, the United States reciprocated.

The "Spanish Protocol" also provided that the U.S. and Egyptian interests sections would retain the ability to communicate directly with their capitals by cipher telegram and diplomatic pouch. Furthermore, the bank accounts in each country previously held by the two embassies were released and put at the disposal of the interests sections. This was a tremendous advantage for the United States. The American government had accumulated, largely through sales of agricultural commodities to Egypt under Public Law 480, Egyptian pound balances totaling the equivalent of hundreds of millions of dollars. Moreover, as the U.S. interests section disposed of surplus property in Egypt our local currency balances grew and grew, despite our tapping them for day-to-day official expenses. Thus in terms of communications and direct access to funds, the two interests sections were in the same position as regular embassies.

Another provision of the "Spanish Protocol" envisaged the eventual reopening of the American consulate general in Alexandria and consulate in Port Said. (For the record, the United States had included the Port Said consulate in the "Spanish Protocol," but with the Suez Canal closed, its east bank occupied by the Israelis, we had little interest in pressing for the reopening of that office.)

This was the one measure provided for in the agreement that was never implemented. In February 1968, the American government informed the Egyptians that we intended to reopen the Alexandria consulate general in modest quarters with a very small staff. At the time the Egyptian Foreign Ministry was informed they interposed no objection. Within hours, however, we were asked urgently to suspend our plans "for the time being." The reason behind the Egyptian *volte face* was quite obvious. Alexandria was the port through which the Russians were carrying out their massive rearmament of Egypt. Moreover, it provided what the Egyptians called "facilities" for the Soviet Mediterranean Fleet. Soviet lack of enthusiasm for an official American presence in that city was, perhaps, understandable.

The writer of this article arrived in Cairo on August 3, 1967, to take charge as principal officer of the U.S. interests section. As has been shown above, the task of establishing the section, clearing away the administrative burden of liquidating a large embassy, and organizing day-to-day operations in a new setting had by then been largely accomplished by the Americans who had stayed behind in June and by Spanish Ambassador Sagaz y Zubelzu. What had not yet begun were substantive conversations with Egyptian officials in Cairo about *the* pressing problem of the Middle East, i.e., dealing with the aftermath of the June war and replacing the previously unstable armistice regime with a structure of permanent peace.

There was a very good reason for this. The center of this activity had been the United Nations in New York, and there the American and Egyptian delegations were in close contact. Despite the rupture of relations, meetings were taking place between the two governments at a ministerial level. Unfortunately these early efforts in the United Nations came to naught, and key Egyptian officials were beginning to return to Cairo by the end of July. The question in our minds was whether, in present circumstances, a direct dialogue could continue between Egyptians and Americans in their respective capitals, away from the United Nations. The answer was not long in coming.

The Spanish ambassador took me to call on the chief of protocol at the Foreign Ministry on August 5. The protocol chief mentioned that an old friend, Mohamed Riad, *chef du cabinet* to the foreign minister, was hoping we could get together. Upon leaving the ministry I telephoned Riad and we met for dinner that night. This was the first of many contacts. For another couple of months, meetings between American diplomats and their Egyptian counterparts took place under the guise of social encounters in private residences. By November, the Egyptians had decided that this was too cumbersome a procedure and began to invite U.S. representatives to call at the Foreign Ministry. Old contacts with officials at the Egyptian Presidency and with influential private Egyptians were resumed with cordiality. On January 6, 1968, I had an unpublicized meeting with President Nasser.

By mid-February 1968, it seemed likely that formal diplomatic relations would shortly be resumed. In an interview with *Look* magazine, Nasser had said that the charge of U.S. complicity in the June War was based on misinformation. The American nonofficial community had by and large returned to Egypt and resumed normal activities. The American University in Cairo, while under formal sequestration, was operating freely and normally. The Pan American Oil Company (a subsidiary of Amoco) was producing oil in the Gulf of Suez and providing much needed oil and foreign exchange to the Egyptians. The American elementary and high schools in Cairo and Alexandria had resumed operations. The resident American press corps in Cairo, as well as visiting correspondents and broadcasters, were getting normal treatment from Egyptian authorities. Diplomatic conversations between the United States and Egypt had greatly intensified since the UN General Assembly had passed a resolution in November 1967 aimed at a peaceful settlement of the Palestine conflict. Egypt had accepted this resolution. A UN mediatory process under Dr. Gunnar Jarring, a senior Swedish diplomat, was under way.

The process of normalization was to be stymied, however, by developments from a wholly unexpected quarter. A court-martial involving the top officers of the Egyptian Air Force got under way early in 1968. The top officers were charged with negligence and incompetence in permitting the destruction of

Egypt's military capability in the air. They were convicted but were given relatively light sentences. This action broke the calm that had existed among the Egyptian people for the long months since the defeat. Demonstrations and riots involving students and workers erupted in Cairo and Alexandria.

The government was surprised and shaken by these events. It promised to retry the officers, to hold new elections "from the bottom to the top" and to institute reforms. At the same time, Nasser caused the press to carry stories to the effect that there would be no change in the U.S.–Egyptian relationship. As he himself explained to us later, he believed that a resumption of diplomatic relations in those circumstances would not have any "popular basis" in Egypt. Formal relations had to await another six years and another Arab-Israel war.

Despite the absence of formal diplomatic relations, diplomatic activity between Egypt and the United States intensified over the period. In the early summer of 1970, Nasser called on the United States to take a new step toward peace. Nasser subsequently agreed, amid much publicity, to a U.S. proposal for a cease-fire along the Suez Canal. An American cabinet officer, the Honorable Elliot Richardson, headed a distinguished official delegation to Nasser's funeral in October of that year. By early 1971, the principal officer of the U.S. interests section was being summoned on a regular basis to meetings with President Anwar el-Sadat. In 1971, the U.S. secretary of state and the Egyptian foreign minister exchanged visits to each other's capitals. Finally, after the 1973 "Yom Kippur War," extensive negotiations took place between President Sadat and Secretary of State Henry Kissinger, which led to the first Egyptian-Israeli disengagement agreement in early 1974. It was only after this step had been accomplished that formal diplomatic relations were resumed in February of that year.

Why were traditional diplomatic patterns and practices so adapted to circumstances in the years 1967 to 1974? The answer is simple. Despite the animosities on both sides that followed the June 1967 war, neither the United States nor Egypt had any real interest in letting contact decline to a formal and indirect level. Egypt did not want to be alone with the Soviet Union. For the United States to seek to protect and promote its interests in the Arab world while ignoring Egypt would have resembled an effort to stage Hamlet with "the character of the Prince of Denmark being left out."

This adaptability, this useful pragmatism in the U.S.–Egyptian relationship during seven years, would not have been possible without the understanding and support of America's protecting power, Spain. An insistence on a rigid adherence to protocol and traditional diplomatic practice would not have advanced the cause of peace in the Eastern Mediterranean, an objective which Spain enthusiastically shared with us. For our part, we viewed our relationship with Spain in this endeavor in Egypt as a genuine opportunity for cooperation. It was standard procedure for us to share confidences across the board with the representative of the protecting power. We undertook early in the process that the Spanish ambassador would never be surprised or caught off guard by any action we took. Mutual consultation was informal, but systematic and comprehensive. Nor was it a one-way street. The Spanish ambassador was highly regarded in Egypt and had many sources of information. The United States never had cause to regret its frank disclosures to our protecting power of a whole range of matters, including the most sensitive ones.

The U.S.–Spanish relationship in Egypt from 1967 to 1974 may have bent a few precedents. Let us hope that it may have established a few new ones. It was an unqualified success.

Annex

NOTE VERBALE

1.–The Embassy of Spain in Cairo presents its compliments to the Ministry of Foreign Affairs and has the honor of bringing to its notice that the United States of America Interests Section of the Spanish Embassy confirms the facilities which have been agreed on the basis of reciprocity as a result of the rupture of Diplomatic relations between the United Arab Republic and the United States of America on the sixth of June, 1967, at 7 p.m. Cairo time.

2.–At the request of the United States Government and with the consent of the United Arab Republic Government, the Embassy of Spain in Cairo undertakes to protect United States interests in the United Arab Republic.

3.–All members of the former United States Embassy have left the United Arab Republic except for the first secretary Mr. William B. Bromell, who remains at present in charge of the United States Section at the Embassy of Spain in Cairo. His name will be inserted in the Diplomatic list as shown in annex 1.

4.–To facilitate the running of the United States Interests Section by its own officers, the United States Government can appoint three diplomatic officers in the United States Interests Section not objected to by the United Arab Republic. These persons as well as the person mentioned in the previous paragraph and members of their families will continue to enjoy the privileges and immunities that are enjoyed by diplomatic members of the Spanish Embassy. Their names will be inserted in the diplomatic list at the end of the list of members of the Embassy of Spain. Two of these officers were retained from the former United States Embassy as shown in annex 1.

5.–In addition, eight administrative officers and two households[1] not objected to by the United Arab Republic, can be affected by the United States Government to work in the United States Interests Section. At present, two of the administrative officers were retained from the former United States Embassy. Their names are given in annex II.

6.–The eight administrative officers and the two households will receive the same treatment as their colleagues in the Embassy of Spain.

7.–The United States Government may, with the prior approval of the Ministry of Foreign Affairs of the United Arab Republic, replace any member of the United States Interests Section or Consulates who leaves the United Arab Republic on transfer or for any other reason.

8.–The United Arab Republic allows the United States Interests Section the freedom in official communications which is set out in the Vienna Convention on Diplomatic Relations. The said Section can contact the local competent authorities regarding United States interests in the United Arab Republic.

9.–The United Arab Republic allows the United States Interests Section to maintain:
   a. a diplomatic bag service.
   b. cypher communications.

10.–The rupture of diplomatic relations does not affect Consular relations between the two countries, nor shall it affect the rights, privileges and immunities, on the basis of reciprocity, accruing from such Consular relations. The United States may continue, on the basis of reciprocity, its Consulate General at Alexandria and its Consulate in Port Said. Their American staff is limited, as agreed upon, to two consular officers and one administrative officer for the first, and one consular officer and one administrative officer for the second. Their names will be subject to approval by the United Arab Republic.

11.–The Consular and Administrative officers shall, on the basis of reciprocity, have the privileges and immunities which are set out in the Vienna Convention on Consular Relations.

Moreover, the consular establishments shall have communications facilities, courier and mail services and may continue all normal consular functions.

12.–The consulates may continue to occupy United States Government owned or leased buildings. But the use of flags and emblems by the American Consulates either at Alexandria or Port Said will be subject of separate negotiations.

13.–All existing international agreements between the United Arab Republic and the United States of America in which the United States Embassy is referred to shall be applied as if these references were to the United States Interests Section of the Spanish Embassy.

14.–The Bank accounts of the former United States Embassy remain unblocked and shall be available for use as hitherto; these accounts shall, however, be designated as accounts of the United States Interests Section of the Spanish Embassy.

15.–The Embassy of Spain avails itself of this opportunity to renew to the Ministry of Foreign Affairs the assurances of its highest consideration.

Cairo, 24 June, 1967

MINISTRY OF FOREIGN AFFAIRS—CAIRO.

ANNEX I

Mr. William B. BROMELL	:	First Secretary (Consular Affairs)
Mr. Martin ARMSTRONG	:	Second Secretary (Administrative Affairs)
Mr. Richard WEITZEL	:	Assistant Attaché (Financial Affairs)

ANNEX II

Mr. Lee GRAHAM

Mr. Roger HYDE

6

The Interests Section as a Practical System of Diplomatic Contact
Egyptian–U.S. Relations at the Time of No Relations, 1967–1974

Ashraf Ghorbal, member of the Egyptian foreign service and former ambassador to the United States (1973–84), was head of the Egyptian interests section in Washington under the Indian flag during the period 1968–72.

EXPERIENCE THROUGHOUT HISTORY HAS SHOWN THAT governments find it easier to break diplomatic relations than to restore them. Usually they resort to a break in a fit of anger or frustration. It is only after the break that they wake up to the result of their action and find themselves in real need of some form of contact, direct or indirect. To meet this need, interests sections have become a medium for diplomatic contact.

Countries that quarrel with each other and reach the point of breaking off diplomatic relations are not aware of the damage they do to themselves, because it is precisely at times of estrangement that relations are needed most. A dialogue is essential, and talking back and forth is the only way to clear a complicated situation. But whether they like it or not, countries do retain the right of severing diplomatic relations when they find no other way.

In its origin, the protecting power system grew out of the need to safeguard the nationals of one country in the land of the other in the absence of diplomatic relations. As such, the system tended to deal more with consular affairs than political matters. In today's world, the need for political dialogue is the *raison d'être* for the establishment of interests sections as part of a protecting power embassy. This is exactly what happened between Egypt and the United States as a result of the 1967 war.

Extremely upset about the Israeli attack in Sinai and its quick success in destroying Egypt's air force, and convinced that Israel had received support from the United States in various ways to be able to achieve such results, Gamal Abdel Nasser decided to sever diplomatic relations with Washington.

Towards the end of May, Nasser was told by the Russians and Syrians that Israel was massing troops along the Israeli-Syrian borders. Arab broadcasts were beaming accusations that Nasser was shielding himself behind United Nations forces. How could he, the leader of Arab liberation and the champion of Arab freedom be so accused? He asked U Thant to pull out the United Nations forces. The message was sent via General Mohamed Fawzi, the minister of defence. Foreign Minister Mahmoud Riad learnt about it after the event. Nasser felt he had to take what appeared to him as the logical follow-up step. When U Thant pointed out that he could not pull out UNEF Forces from Sinai and leave them in Sharm El Sheikh, Nasser called on U Thant to pull them out equally from Sharm El Sheikh and closed the Gulf of Aqaba to Israeli shipping. This is exactly what Israel wanted to happen to claim a *casus belli*. Israel pre-empted with its blow on 5 June.

Many analysts have since debated the question: did Nasser really want to go to war? As I lived closely these events, I am convinced he did not.

Nasser banked more on the diplomatic way out, a repeat of 1956. He was pleased that President Johnson offered to send his vice president, Hubert Humphrey, to both Egypt and Israel to mediate the problem. Nasser, as a gesture in response, offered also to send his vice president, Zakaria Mohieddin, to Washington. To him this contained enough of a message of readiness to deescalate, to play ball and seek a way out of the impasse. I share the view of many who feel that it is precisely because of that that Israel decided to pre-empt. To her this was a golden opportunity to direct a blow to the Egyptian armed forces. Israel did not hesitate, and strike on 5 June she did.

What made matters worse was the behavior of the Egyptian military command. Through bungling, Egypt's air force remained on the ground. It became an easy target for the Israeli air force. Neither the Egyptian armour nor infantry had a chance to fight. An untimely withdrawal was ordered with the forces leaving their gear behind. It was agonizing and humiliating. The defeat was quick.

Whatever the truth about the U.S. role then, and whether Nasser's accusations were correct or wrong, what matters to us in this context is to state that as soon as the break was decided politically, the need arose technically to maintain a dialogue between Cairo and Washington. Although at first the Ministry of Foreign Affairs in Cairo recommended that twelve diplomats remain on each side in interests sections, Nasser, as part of the political posture decided upon, reduced the number to five. That was a further expression of Nasser's dismay with Washington.

It was not long after the break that Donald Bergus returned to Cairo as head of the U.S. interests section within the Spanish embassy. He had spent three years as political counselor in the U.S. embassy in Cairo till shortly before the war. He was a familiar figure there. I went to Washington some five months later, attached formally to the Indian embassy.

Why did Egypt choose India in particular to look after her interests in the American capital? Cairo could not choose an Arab country, for it was expected that all Arab states, in solidarity with Egypt, Jordan, and Syria, the victims of the Israeli aggression, would break en masse with the United States. To name any would be to shed doubt on such expectation. Besides, Cairo was counting on Arab solidarity. If it did not manifest itself to the needed degree at the time of military operations, then at least a break with Washington would convey a serious signal of collective indignation at the U.S. attitude. India, moreover, as one of the three leaders—together with Egypt and Yugoslavia—of the non-aligned movement, was a natural friend from whom to seek help.

The decision proved a wise one, for India enjoyed respect in Washington and elsewhere and her ambassador was highly regarded. The Indians in Washington also proved helpful in terms of providing every opportunity to do what was needed on Egypt's behalf when asked, but leaving us alone to attend to our tasks at other times. They did not insist on playing any role when it was not requested. At the same time, they appreciated being informed about what was going on between the two countries.

Both Bergus and I were advised on arrival in each other's capital that our meetings were to be confined to the chief of protocol or, at most, the head of the country's affairs. But these limitations hardly lasted a day. In theory, the Protocol Office was to arrange and attend every meeting on the substantive side. In practice, Bergus on his side and I on mine touched base with Protocol the first day. On subsequent meetings we just called up our friends, saying can we meet somewhere, in the State Department, the Ministry of Foreign Affairs, or outside.

The personal friendships each of us had opened the doors to a growing number of people with higher responsibilities and wider mandate. I recall Donald Bergus recounting that the week he arrived he dined with Mohamed Riad, my late friend and colleague who was then chief of cabinet of the foreign minister. And I, coming to Washington, was immediately able to see Richard Parker, head of Egyptian affairs, and a few days later dined with Assistant Secretary of State Lucius Battle. Battle had been ambassador to Cairo and had left Egypt some five months before the Israeli oppression. These relationships, I think, did help a great deal in creating clear and healthy channels of communication between the two countries.

Over the months and years I spent in Washington as head of the interests section (January 1968–July 1972), I was lucky to be counted among the most persistent Arab envoys to knock on the doors of the State Department, the National Security Council, even the Pentagon, notwithstanding the close military relationship Egypt had at the time with the Soviet Union while the U.S. fully backed Israel. I made clear to Cairo that I intended to pursue every avenue, and not to confine myself to the State Department. I was determined to develop contacts with the Pentagon as a participant in the making of U.S. foreign policy. Moreover, I knocked on the gates of the Congress to try to see congressmen and senators in the hope of impressing upon them our desire for a peaceful solution. Many encouraged my effort.

I must admit it was not easy to start with Egypt having the image it had. When I arrived in Washington in January 1968, Cairo's image was that of an aggressor, even though we were the victims of Israeli attack and our land was under Israeli occupation. But the brinkmanship of Nasser in calling on U Thant to withdraw UN forces from Sinai and Sharm El Sheikh had left behind a negative imprint that cost Egypt much needed support. Not many had bothered to look at the root of the trouble, and many had been influenced by a systematic campaign to portray Israel as a victim. Israel enjoyed a special status thanks to a very strong and effective lobby. What Israel asked for, Israel received: money, weapons, and political support. What Israel did not ask for was voluntarily offered to her. I discovered that many Jewish congressmen and senators felt that they had a sacred mission to help Israel and provide her with what they perceived as necessary for her security and well-being, even military power that far exceeded her needs.

In their eyes, the Arabs in general and Nasser's Egypt in particular were villains, and such a powerful lobby was not going to hide its feelings. Many other congressmen felt we had a legitimate case to present, but we had to realize that the Arab lobby, Arab influence, is hardly existent, let alone felt. Thus, it was not easy to secure a meeting with some legislators. Some

Arab ambassadors whose countries maintained diplomatic relations with Washington helped provide opportunities for meetings. The late Abdel Hamid Sharif, ambassador of Jordan, later his country's prime minister, as well as Sheikh Salem Al Sabah, ambassador of Kuwait, later minister of defence and then of interior in Kuwait, were particularly helpful. I accompanied them to many meetings they had on Capitol Hill. Thus not only were our views aired, but a high degree of Arab solidarity was manifested from such meetings. This is not to mention the opportunities provided in social gatherings.

I was determined, with the full blessings of my government, to carry our voice and views to everyone I could reach, and definitely to the media. That was perhaps the hardest.

Many people in the media gave me the opportunity to make our case known. They welcomed someone who could talk to them and explain. I discovered that if you put your case logically, there is a possibility that it will get into print. I could not make an impact the first time, but I tried again and again. It was quite an effort, but a rewarding one. My relationship with the media convinced me that one has to tell them the truth, whatever it is, and if one could not, then silence is the essence of wisdom. They respected one's inability to speak at times. Most important, I was convinced one should not give them an untrue story because they will find out the truth and expose it. Worse, one would lose credibility.

Needless to say, one cannot expect to have an immediate impact. One is in a continuous educational process, explaining over and over again to the media the philosophy of one's country, why you are doing what. It was not easy when, for instance, an extremist group would threaten to blow up a plane, as happened in Amman, or a certain plane was hijacked. One is automatically questioned as if one had committed the act oneself. When we were receiving arms from the Soviets to defend ourselves, every time an article appeared, in whichever paper, it contained such references as "an Egyptian carrying a Russian Kalashnikov." Always Egyptian coupled with Russian. It became a sort of image association. We needed to explain that we were not communists, but were being helped by whoever would give us the means to defend ourselves. It was not easy, but we could still get a fair hearing at times, though definitely not frequently.

On the economic side of the relationship, United States investments in Egypt in 1967 were not great enough to make much difference when relations were broken. Our oil was yet to be discovered in large quantities, whereas today it comprises a big portion of our exports to the United States. Amoco (formerly Standard Oil of Indiana) had just made its first major discoveries. Its operations proceeded smoothly. Both sides were anxious to help this joint venture develop further. Amoco's representative in Cairo, James Vanderbeek, was even decorated by Nasser for a job well done.

In 1967 textiles were the main export item to the United States. Trade was mostly in American exports to Egypt, industrial as well as agricultural. These continued within the limited financial means at the disposal of Egypt, although there was no credit. Wheat, which was a primary item of U.S. assistance to Egypt, had been stopped. This withholding of assistance was in fact a triggering factor in the worsening of relations prior to the break of diplomatic relations. Nasser considered such a sudden stop, especially in food for the masses, as a twisting of the arm, an attitude he resented immensely. So by the time relations were severed, economic and commercial relations had very much shrunk.

On the other hand, cultural relations remained active. The American University in Cairo had no problem. It continued without interruption. Egyptian students enrolled in U.S. universities continued their studies without any trouble.

The combined efforts of the two interest sections should have kept each capital fully informed of the views or reactions of the other. Being the only conduit between the two countries gave us a degree of "importance" different from that enjoyed by ambassadors exchanged during normal relations, when messages are frequently and directly exchanged between foreign ministers or even heads of state, who may communicate personally by telephone.

Bergus and I were sometimes accused of doing such a thorough job that we hurt the need for an earlier resumption of relations! While it was massaging to one's ego to hear such praise, it was definitely a gross exaggeration. Countries resume diplomatic relations for important political considerations. When these are at hand, or at least anticipated, then the step is taken regardless of personnel questions.

But personal relations had their value nonetheless. At one point, a distinguished ambassador of a friendly country advised me to urge my government to resume relations with Washington without delay, as that would be beneficial to our cause. He was somewhat apologetic, explaining that it was not meant as a reflection on my effort, but he was convinced that it is easier for an ambassador in a situation of normal diplomatic relations to see the secretary of state or the national security adviser; in case a meeting is not quickly set up, the ambassador can seek the intervention of his government. A few weeks later, we both attended a reception at the Soviet embassy, where Henry Kissinger and I shook hands and talked for a while. Later this same ambassador inquired of me what Kissinger had talked about. When I answered, truthfully, that he had asked me to go and see him, the ambassador just looked at me, turned around, and left.

As a general rule, diplomats, in the exercise of their duties, find that they cannot always rely solely on instructions from their government. One must also rely on one's sense of appraisal of the situation at hand and act without hesitation, as long as one does so within the frame of his government's policy. I found from experience, however, that during times of no relations this is more frequently needed than during times of normal and friendly relations. I recall how sometimes I woke up in the morning to hear on the radio that there was a statement coming out from Cairo which the radio described negatively. In my judgment, it was important that it be read within its proper context. Here the element of time was vital.

I never hesitated to call up Assistant Secretary of State Joseph Sisco at seven o'clock in the morning when needed, suggesting breakfast at his place or mine.

I did not feel in these situations that I had to wait for Cairo to give me instructions, for it was in such encounters that one tried to prevent an over-reaction. It is essential, in my estimation, that diplomats have the initiative and play an active role at such times.

During the transition after the election of President Nixon in 1968, I went to see Foreign Minister Mahmoud Riad, who was attending the UN General Assembly in New York. I raised with him the question of resumption of relations. I was trying to find the proper timing and formula. I thought that to trigger such a step, President Nixon might be persuaded to include in his inaugural speech something that could justify such an action by Nasser. Riad had no objection, stating that I had created an assignment for myself. I conveyed my idea to former World Bank President Eugene Black, who liked it and suggested I go home and do my homework and write something he could carry to the President-elect. Perhaps one day, he said, you will tell your children and grandchildren you helped the President of the United States write his inaugural speech. I went home and wrote what I thought would get relations moving. I gave my draft to Gene Black, and we called it "the Black paper for a white purpose." To our surprise and dismay, President Nixon talked in his inaugural address only about concepts, and not about problems and regions. So that chance for a resumption of relations evaporated.

Although personal friendship plays a significant part in such circumstances, I never lost sight of the fact that the two countries, Egypt and the United States, are very important to each other. For Egypt, the United States has always been very important. The United States is not only a superpower, but a country we need to have, if not on our side, then at least as a fair go-between to help bring about a just settlement to the Middle East problem—Sadat used to call the United States the partner in the peace process. This is not to mention the technology and the assistance we need from the United States.

On the other hand, though Egypt is a small country, it is a leader in its area and in the non-aligned movement. Suffice to recall that even in the absence of diplomatic relations, Secretary of State William P. Rogers visited Cairo in 1971 and Foreign Minister Riad visited Washington the same year. This is not to mention the multiple times the two met in New York at the UN General Assembly. And President Nasser corresponded with President Lyndon Johnson in 1968 and even sent Dr. Mohamed Fawzi, former minister of foreign affairs, to attend President Eisenhower's funeral in Washington, where he was received by President Nixon. There were high expectations in Washington that this would signal a readiness to reestablish relations. Fawzi did recommend it, but Nasser did not find the timing right.

In February 1973, as part of a program of visits to the capitals of the five great powers, President Sadat sent his national security advisor, Hafez Ismail, to meet with President Nixon. Ismail also had a long and extensive discussion with Henry Kissinger at that time in Armonk, New York, and again in Paris in April of that year, in both instances seeking, behind the scenes, a way out of the Middle East impasse. Egypt was trying its best to convince the Nixon administration to put pressure on Israel to come to an honorable settlement. But as Kissinger admits in his book *Years of Upheaval*, he was convinced that Egypt had no military option and thus no choice but to accept Israel's terms in direct negotiations. Six months later, he knew very well he had been mistaken. The Suez Canal was crossed, the Israeli Bar-Lev line stormed, and Egypt's image totally changed. The October War had to happen for the United States to reassess its policy.

―――――――――――

Throughout the 1967–74 period of the interests sections, my relations with the Indian ambassadors in Washington were very cordial and of valued reward (in particular with Ali Jawer Jung, a dear friend from his days as India's ambassador to Cairo). Not only were they always anxious to give of their vital advice and rich experience; but also, when they intervened on our behalf, it was with the weight and importance of India. We worked from our own chancery and lived in our own residence, with only our stationery under the seal of the Indian embassy and the buildings flying the Indian flag. At first, when the switchboard operator began by answering "Indian Embassy," the callers would hang up before hearing "Egyptian Interests Section." Once we reversed the order, the callers stayed on the line.

At times of difficulties between countries, a normal diplomatic relationship is always preferable. Where none exists, however, the interests section has proven its value as a channel of communications. During much of the 1980s, Egypt had no diplomatic relations with twenty Arab states. Yet in each Egypt was represented, and vice versa, by an interests section headed by a diplomat of the grade of ambassador, with access to the head of state of the host country.

Interests sections have indeed become another diplomatic medium—necessary and practical as long as states have reason to exercise their right to break diplomatic relations, but realize they cannot totally do away with a dialogue. The need for direct communication remains. Indeed, it is the essence of wisdom to say that it is during a break of diplomatic relations that countries most need close contacts.

7

Evolution of the U.S. Interests Sections in Algiers and Baghdad

William Eagleton

William Eagleton is uniquely qualified to comment on U.S. relations with countries officially unfriendly to the United States. Not only did he serve as chief of interests sections during breaks in diplomatic relations with Iraq and Algeria; he also served as chargé d'affaires in Libya just before the United States withdrew its embassy from that country. He later became U.S. ambassador to Syria.

MY SERVICE WITH U.S. INTERESTS SECTIONS OCCURRED WHEN I headed USINT Algiers, 1969–74, under the Swiss flag, and USINT Baghdad, 1980–84, under the Belgian flag. The operations of these two offices were in most respects similar.

Because at the time of the "Six-Day War" in 1967 the Algerian and Iraqi governments had broken relations with the United States, the U.S. position was that relations could be restored at any time without precondition. This attitude caused the United States to be more inclined than the host country to upgrade the status of the interests section, provided that any changes would be reciprocal. Such a gradual process did, in fact, take place in Algiers, and later in Baghdad, so that by the

---

The views expressed in this chapter do not necessarily reflect those of the U.S. Department of State.

time full diplomatic relations were restored, little more was needed than assigning ambassadors and changing flags and stationery.

The interests sections were, for the most part, treated as if they were embassies. In Algeria, our consulates in Oran and Constantine remained open and functioned normally, since consular relations had not been broken. The head of the interests section was invited to all national day receptions, except those of countries with which the United States did not have diplomatic relations. He was also invited to ceremonies and functions given by the host government at which the diplomatic corps was present. This included airport arrivals of VIP's, host country national day receptions, and other such events. At private functions hosted by Algerians and Iraqis, the Americans were treated much like other foreign diplomats. In those two countries, invitations to private homes were not numerous.

It is my recollection that in both Algeria and Iraq, there was an understanding regarding the size of our respective interests sections. In both cases, we were told at an early stage that the host government would be prepared on a reciprocal basis to increase the number of persons assigned to the sections. This we did, although modestly.

During my service in Algiers and Baghdad there were no notable manifestations of hostility toward the interests sections or their personnel. We were subject to the same travel procedures that applied to all other foreign diplomats (since we were technically diplomats of the Swiss and Belgian embassies). In both cases, this required submitting forms with travel plans ahead of time and receiving permission from the Foreign Ministry.

The Algerian and Iraqi governments operated their interests sections in Washington much as we did ours in their capitals; that is, they functioned much as embassies do. However, most high-level contact and dialogue took place in Algiers and Baghdad rather than in Washington.

Algiers, 1969–1974

Relations with the Host Country

By the time I arrived in Algiers in November 1969, the U.S. interests section of the Swiss embassy had been in existence for more than two years. At no time had U.S. personnel been completely removed from Algiers. Instead, a small American contingent remained when the embassy was officially closed, functioning as an interests section of the Swiss embassy. This "section" occupied, or at least maintained, all the properties of the U.S. embassy. No Swiss citizens were assigned to the section. The first chief of the U.S. interests section, Lewis Hoffacker, had been deputy chief of mission of the embassy at the time of the break in relations.

When I arrived in Algiers, I found the interests section operating like an embassy, but with a number of handicaps. For example, we lacked the high-level contact with the Algerian government that the situation warranted. Furthermore, the interests section had no defense attaché's office, though it did have a small U.S. Information Service [USIS] cultural program.

My contacts at the Foreign Ministry initially centered on the chief of protocol and his assistants. The Algerian side appeared to consider this a more appropriate way to communicate than through political offices. Nevertheless, we soon developed midlevel contacts on the political side and established a close and useful relationship with a senior official in the presidency who acted as President Houari Boumediene's *chef de cabinet* for political affairs.

In 1969, one of the anomalies in our written communications with the Algerian government was that all of our diplomatic notes, however trivial, were taken from the embassy at the top of the hill overlooking Algiers Bay, down to the Swiss embassy in the port area for initialing, and then back up the hill to the Algerian Foreign Ministry. This operation added at least a day each way in communicating with the ministry. Soon after my arrival, the Foreign Ministry agreed that we could send our notes directly to the ministry, a matter of a few blocks. As I recall, the letterhead of these notes read, "The American Interests Section of the Swiss Embassy."

The move toward de facto full relations was a gradual one, stimulated by Algeria's desire to increase technological and economic ties with the United States, particularly in the field of liquified natural gas [LNG]. To finance their large LNG project required American government participation in the form of an Export-Import Bank loan. My first meeting with Foreign Minister Abdelaziz Bouteflika (at his request) occurred about a year after my arrival, and the subject of the meeting was U.S. financing for the El Paso LNG project. The El Paso project was a major U.S. investment designed to process Algerian natural gas for export to Europe and the United States. It involved extensive negotiations over the Export-Import Bank financing for the plant and ships.

As commercial and technological relations increased, so did the flow of American visitors. Contacts then developed at the ministerial level, not as courtesy calls but in connection with specific projects. The first U.S. contacts at the presidential level were made by several presidents of U.S. companies and banks. The chief of USINT did not sit in on these meetings, but was active in the background.

Throughout the period from 1970 to 1974, we were in touch with the Algerian presidency on a number of subjects, including the Vietnam war (the Algerians were among those contacted in connection with U.S. prisoners in North Vietnam) and the Arab-Israeli dispute. Before and following the October 1973 Arab-Israeli war, Secretary of State Henry Kissinger was exchanging messages with the Algerian leadership through "pieces of paper" passed by the chief of USINT to the Algerian presidency. Later that year and again in the spring of 1974, Dr. Kissinger visited Algiers and met with President Boumediene. By the time I left Algiers in June 1974, I had had two meetings with Boumediene, both of which were publicized in the Algerian media.

In the spring of 1974, President Boumediene, while in New York at a special session of the UN General Assembly, was invited to Washington, where he met, and later dined, with President Nixon. All of this illustrates how little impediment there is to top-level contact between countries lacking diplomatic relations, provided both sides agree that such contacts are desirable.

Relations with the Protecting Power

In Algiers, the relationship between the U.S. interests section and its protecting embassy and ambassador was similar to that between two embassies that enjoy special and friendly ties. At no time during my tour of four and a half years in Algiers did the Swiss ambassador, of which there were three in that period, approach the Algerian government on behalf of the United States. I kept the Swiss ambassador informed of the anticipated arrival of high-level U.S. visitors to Algiers and other items that would interest him as protecting ambassador. However, this was more a courtesy than a requirement. During Secretary of State Kissinger's visits, the Swiss ambassador played no substantive role. The Algerians made it clear that they preferred it that way.

As an interests section, we flew the Swiss flag on the roof of the chancery. When I arrived, I found a Swiss flag also on the ambassador's residence near the chancery, and it remained there until renewal of relations. Its presence was probably not correct, since there can be only one Swiss ambassador in Algiers and he would fly the flag at his residence. The initial placement of the flag there might have been considered an additional means of protecting that prime property. The U.S. interests section during the period, with about fifteen American employees, was more than twice the size of the Swiss embassy.

USINT Algiers on the Local Scene

The interests section in Algiers was treated by resident diplomatic missions very much like an embassy headed by a chargé d'affaires *ad interim*. Thus, the chief of USINT stood in the protocol rank below the ambassadors, and in Algiers even below the chargés d'affaires. Given the importance of the United States, this lowly position became almost a privileged one, since it set the American representative apart from the others. This position also simplified diplomatic calls, since it permitted the chief of USINT to make the first call on a newly arrived ambassador without awaiting the ambassador's mutual courtesy call. Seating of the chief of USINT and his wife at dinner parties was an advantage to their diplomatic hosts because it permitted them to fill in the middle of the table at dinners attended mainly by ambassadors.

When I arrived in Algiers in 1969, it was my understanding that the Algerian government did not wish us to host the traditional Fourth of July reception for the diplomatic corps, Algerian officials, and friends. Hence, we organized the residence garden picnics for the three hundred to four hundred Americans in Algiers. At that time, a large American flag was draped over the building and at noon the national anthem was played. As relations improved and holding a normal reception became feasible (I believe the Algerians meanwhile were holding receptions in Washington on their national day), I took the position that until we had full diplomatic relations, with our flag flying, we would not host a national day reception but would continue our all-American picnics. These were enlarged by inviting the British and French ambassadors, and finally a representative of the Foreign Ministry, to be present at the noon ceremony. These celebrations in Algiers were among the most successful, and certainly the most emotional, I have ever witnessed. The ban on flying the flag throughout the year made it all the more dramatic when the flag appeared on the Fourth and the national anthem was played.

In 1973, the Algerian government indicated that it would consider our participation at the Algerian International Trade Fair a positive gesture. The American pavilion, although not the largest, was given equal treatment with the others, flying the American flag and hosting a walk-through by President

Boumediene on opening day. By this time relations were virtually normal in everything but name, though the official renewal of relations did not occur until late 1974.

Baghdad, 1980–1984

Relations with the Host Country

My experience in upgrading the U.S. interests section in Algiers was repeated during the 1980–84 period in Baghdad. The history of our Baghdad break [recounted in chapter 4] and the establishment of the interests section there, however, were somewhat different. The 1967 break in Baghdad was total, with the removal of all American personnel and the occupation of our large new embassy compound by a representative of the protecting power, Belgium. This caretaker status lasted until October 1972, when we sent a few American personnel back to Baghdad. They did not occupy the old embassy, which had meanwhile been taken over by the Iraqi government for use as a foreign ministry, but rather relocated in a modest building in the residential area of Baghdad.

USINT Baghdad was then about the same size as the Belgian embassy, that is, a chief and several American officers and a handful of clerical personnel and communicators. By 1980, there were about fifteen Americans in USINT, as compared to about five Belgians in the Belgian embassy. Contacts with the Iraqi government were infrequent and were conducted at midlevel. Communication with the State Department was via telex rather than radio. Permission to operate our own radio was obtained shortly after my arrival.

Drawing on experience from Algiers, we worked to upgrade the status of the interests section during a period when U.S.–Iraqi relations were themselves gradually improving. In 1982, President Saddam Hussein let it be known that the U.S. interests section would thereafter be treated like an embassy and the chief of USINT like an ambassador. Our contacts quickly expanded laterally and upward, though within the rather strict confines set for all diplomatic missions by the Iraqi authorities.

In 1983, Iraq assigned a senior party official well connected within the Iraqi government as chief of the Iraqi Interests Section in Washington. Thereafter his efforts to upgrade the status of our interests sections were, if anything, greater than mine. They were certainly more effective, since his government could set the pace knowing we would follow. By the end of 1983, high-level American visitors to Baghdad were being received by President Hussein. When the United States and Iraq resumed full diplomatic relations in November 1984, the U.S. interests section was raised to embassy status and David G. Newton, head of the section, became chargé d'affaires *ad interim* (and, the following summer, ambassador).

Relations with the Protecting Power

Relations between USINT Baghdad and the Belgian embassy were similar to those I had encountered in Algiers. I believe that, at the request of the Belgian embassy, the letterhead on the stationery featured "Embassy of Belgium" in large print with "U.S. Interests Section" in small letters. Our notes to the Foreign Ministry initially were addressed from "the Belgian Embassy, U.S. Interests Section," but later read "U.S. Interests Section of the Belgian Embassy." These nuances may or may not have been significant, depending on how they were interpreted by other embassies and the Foreign Ministry.

USINT Baghdad's Status on the Local Scene

In Baghdad there was no flag over the residence, though the Belgian flag flew over the "chancery." The chief of USINT in Baghdad was, at the time of my arrival, treated more as an ambassador than had been the case in Algiers. For example, when the dean of the diplomatic corps gave his traditional farewell reception for departing ambassadors, the chief of USINT was invited to participate and to contribute the standard fee for the farewell present. He in turn received his farewell reception and a gift on his departure. (In Algiers, the Chief of USINT did not contribute or have his own farewell reception. However, as a courtesy, the dean, the Saudi ambassador, invited him to all farewell receptions.)

Conclusions

As experience in Algiers and Baghdad illustrates, the interests section can function quite satisfactorily as a diplomatic establishment during periods when, for one reason or another, full diplomatic relations have been severed. Not the least of the advantages to a USINT chief is the ease of the assignment process, which involves a routine "paneling" by the State Department, in contrast to the long (six–eight months) and complicated ordeal faced by ambassadorial candidates. In the case of chiefs of interests sections, the simple agreement of the receiving party is all that is required from the host country.

One problem that has never been resolved, however, is the cumbersome title, both of the office itself and the head of that office. "Chief of the United States Interests Section" sounds even worse in French than in English. I recall that the best rendition, though not an officially approved one, occurred at a large reception at the French Embassy in Algiers when I was introduced as *"le réprésentant américain."* Looking back, I wish that it had been possible to use that title during the nine years I spent heading interests sections.

Nevertheless, the experience as a whole was positive, drawing on one's ingenuity and imagination and demonstrating that countries lacking diplomatic relations can, if both desire, maintain high-level contacts and engage in useful dialogues while they await the right moment to renew full diplomatic ties.

8

The Protecting Power and the U.S. Interests Section in Cuba

Wayne S. Smith

Wayne Smith was third secretary of the U.S. embassy in Havana, 1958–61, and chief of the U.S. interests section in Havana, 1979–82. He is now adjunct professor of Latin American studies at the Johns Hopkins University School of Advanced International Studies in Washington, D.C.

THE BREAK IN RELATIONS BETWEEN THE UNITED STATES AND Cuba on January 3, 1961, came as no surprise. Animosity between the two countries had grown steadily since the summer of 1959, so much so that all American dependents had been evacuated in August of 1960 and Ambassador Philip Bonsal recalled in October.

The final strain came in Fidel Castro's speech of January 2, 1961. He described the American embassy as a "nest of spies" and demanded that its staff be reduced to eleven "officials."

Our chargé d'affaires, Daniel Braddock, consulted the Department of State that evening. It was agreed that if the Cubans meant eleven officers of diplomatic rank, the embassy would remain open. If, on the other hand, they defined "official" as any embassy employee, we would be forced to break relations and turn our affairs over to a protecting power. The next morning, the answer came back from the Cuban

Foreign Ministry: "officials" included everyone—code clerks, secretaries, Marine guards, and archivists, as well as diplomats. Thus, on the afternoon of January 3, 1961, the embassy informed the Cuban government that diplomatic relations had ceased to exist. The next day, January 4, the main body of embassy personnel left the country.

The Swiss Take Over

As we moved toward the break, most of us in the embassy had assumed that, when it came, we would turn U.S. interests over to Great Britain, which had the only other embassy in town that seemed large enough to absorb them. To our surprise, the Department of State informed us on January 3 that we would be turning our affairs over to the Swiss. (Cuba would turn its affairs over to the Czech embassy in Washington.) At first, Switzerland seemed a strange choice, for the Swiss embassy in Havana consisted only of the ambassador and one first secretary! As it turned out, however, the Swiss, who are, to put it mildly, experienced in such matters, were to fly in an entire diplomatic team to take over U.S. interests—nine diplomats, headed by an officer of ambassadorial rank. The team arrived on January 7 and received the keys to the U.S. chancery and residence from Chargé d'Affaires Braddock.

From that point in early 1961 until September 1, 1977, Swiss diplomats handled U.S. interests in Cuba. They visited American prisoners, looked after the few American citizens remaining in Cuba, issued visas, and handled communications between the U.S. and Cuban governments. The United States government compensated Switzerland for these and all other services rendered.

Once U.S. diplomatic property had been catalogued and a routine established, the original Swiss team of nine was reduced to three, headed by a first secretary. Although housed in the old U.S. chancery, they became an integral part of the Swiss embassy.

Given the animosity between Washington and Havana, representing U.S. interests in Cuba was often a difficult, unenviable task. Perhaps the harshest times fell to Ambassador Emil Stadelhofer (1963–66). In 1964, because of the arrest of a number of Cuban fishing boats in the Florida Keys, the Cuban government decreed the seizure of the U.S. embassy building and its transformation into the Cuban Ministry of Fishing. Cuban officials appeared at the entrance, determined to take possession, but Ambassador Stadelhofer barred the door. This was diplomatic property, he declared, and would be violated only over his body. The Cubans relented. No further efforts were made to seize the building.

Then came the Camarioca crisis—something of a forerunner of the 1980 Mariel sealift.[1] Castro announced on September 28, 1965, that any Cuban who wished to leave the country was free to do so. They had only to go to the port of Camarioca, a small fishing village just east of Varadero, where friends or relatives from the United States could pick them up by small boat. Over the next few weeks, some five thousand Cubans left for the United States in everything from cabin cruisers to skiffs with outboard motors. Several lost their lives in this impromptu sealift. Other thousands were camped out waiting in Camarioca, while others (no one knows how many) were headed there from all over the island.

With the U.S. Coast Guard warning of a maritime disaster if the sealift was not closed off, and the sudden and uncontrolled departure of people from their jobs threatening a serious impact on the Cuban economy, both governments came to see it in their common interest to halt the sealift and organize an orderly departure program in its place. The result was the Refugee Airlift. This was negotiated with the Cuban government by Ambassador Stadelhofer, who based himself on guidelines and, in some cases, specific instructions from the Department of State. The face-to-face bargaining fell entirely to him, however, and he handled it brilliantly.

Over the next eight years, more than ninety thousand Cubans came to the United States via the Refugee Airlift. All were interviewed and documented by the Swiss in Havana before departure, and every case had to be coordinated with and approved by Washington. Probably no protecting power

has ever before or since shouldered a greater burden. Year
after year, over one thousand Cubans a month were processed
by the Swiss embassy team handling U.S. interests, until Castro
closed down the airlift in 1973, saying it had outlived its
usefulness.

American Diplomats Return to Staff the Interests Section

By 1975, the United States and Cuba were groping toward
rapprochement. Secret talks were begun under the Ford
administration, but broke down over Angola before any
bridges could be built. Ameliorative efforts were resumed
under the Carter administration, which was inaugurated in
January 1977. In March of that year, American and Cuban
diplomats met in New York to discuss maritime boundaries
and fishing rights. In April, they signed agreements on these
issues in Havana. While in the Cuban capital, the chief of the
U.S. delegation, Terence Todman, raised with the Cuban
foreign minister the possibility of opening interests sections in
one another's capitals staffed by Cuban and American diplomats. Subsequently, the Cubans responded enthusiastically to
the idea.

Why did the two sides not simply reestablish diplomatic
relations and open embassies in one another's capitals?
Essentially, because they had taken mutually exclusive positions. Castro had said he wanted to improve relations with the
United States and in principle was prepared to negotiate most
of the major issues between the two countries. He had added,
however, that so long as the U.S. trade embargo against Cuba
was maintained, normal relations could not exist, nor would
Cuba be able to negotiate anything, because the embargo
placed Cuba in an unequal position.

The United States, in turn, took the position that it had not
imposed the trade embargo until Cuba had nationalized all
U.S. properties without compensation. Thus, it could not lift
that embargo until an agreement on compensation had been

reached. But how could they discuss the two problems at all without direct communications?

One might sum up the situation, then, by saying the two sides had ruled out full diplomatic relations until at least two of the major problems between them had been resolved, but in order to discuss possible solutions to these problems, direct and confidential communication was needed. The answer was found in interests sections.

Thus, in May 1977, a U.S. delegation led by Ambassador William Luers and a Cuban delegation led by Vice Minister of Foreign Relations Pelegrín Torras exchanged diplomatic notes in New York providing for the establishment of such sections. Although neither the Swiss nor Czech governments were parties to the exchange of notes, both had been kept fully informed by the U.S. and Cuban governments, respectively, and each had approved the substance of its protected power's note before it went forward.

The basic outline of what was agreed in the exchange of notes was as follows:

—Each interests section could have a staff of up to ten permanent personnel carrying diplomatic or official passports. In addition to these, each section could hire as many citizens of the receiving country as it wished as support staff.
—Each interests section would be housed in its country's former embassy building.
—The respective sections would be part of the Swiss and Czech embassies, but have direct communications with the host government. The highest level at which the chief of the U.S. interests section would be received would be the vice ministerial, and, appropriately, Pelegrín Torras was designated as the vice minister to receive him. The chief of the Cuban interests section could be received by State Department officials up to and including the undersecretary for political affairs.
—The chiefs of the two sections would be invited to all functions for the diplomatic corps and otherwise treated as chiefs

of mission. For protocolary purposes, each would be ranked just after the most junior chargé d'affaires.
—The two sections could perform normal consular functions, such as issuance of passports and visas, and protection of citizens.
—The two sections and their personnel would enjoy all rights, immunities, and privileges normally accorded diplomatic personnel in the two capitals. Neither, however, would fly its own flag or use its own seals.

When studied closely, the two notes clearly outlined a modus operandi in which the two interests sections were to do everything embassies would have done—everything, that is, except fly their colors and call their chiefs "ambassador." It was, in effect, a way of having virtually all the advantages of diplomatic relations without actually acknowledging that they existed.

The two interests sections were inaugurated on September 1, 1977, although diplomats from the respective countries had, in preparation, taken up station in each other's capital several days earlier. Lyle F. Lane was the first chief of the U.S. interests section, serving there from 1977 until 1979. Ramón Sánchez-Parodi was the first chief of the Cuban interests section, serving over eleven years in Washington, until May 1989.

The American Deposits

All during the years that they had handled U.S. interests in Cuba on their own, the Swiss had faithfully accepted and kept for safekeeping the valuables of departing American citizens. Silver, jewelry, paintings, and various other items were considered by the Cuban government to be part of the national patrimony and could not be removed from the country. Rather than leaving them to be confiscated by the government, most Americans deposited them with the Swiss, in the hope that some day they could return to claim them, or that the Cuban government would permit their shipment to the United States.

As we moved to establish an American-staffed section in Havana, the Department of State had two viable options (a third, suggested by the Bureau of Consular Affairs, that we refuse to accept the deposits at all, was not viable): It could leave the deposits where they were (in the old embassy building, which we were now reoccupying), or it could raise the matter with the Cuban government with a view to having them shipped back to the United States for return to their owners—or, in many cases, their heirs.

Because of the opposition of the Bureau of Consular Affairs, which argued that U.S. regulations forbade the acceptance of such deposits and that we would have no legal authority to bring them back to the United States, the second option was rejected and the deposits were left where they were. There, sadly, they remain today, in a vault inside the U.S. interests section. But failure to return them to their owners was in no way the fault of the Swiss. They did their part.

Problems Caused by Worsening U.S.–Cuban Relations

Ironically, no sooner had the interests sections been established in 1977 than U.S.–Cuban relations again began to deteriorate—over Angola, over Cuban support for Puerto Rican independence, and, shortly, over Cuban troops in Ethiopia. Fidel Castro's speeches frequently reflected the rising temper of the times.

This resulted in an interesting situation between the protected and protecting powers. As it had been agreed that the chief of the U.S. interests section would be invited to all functions as though he were chief of mission, Lyle Lane was invited to most functions at which Castro gave speeches— functions such as the 26th of July anniversary ceremonies and major international conferences. On at least two occasions, he found Castro's references to the United States so insulting that he walked out.

Swiss Ambassador Jean-Pierre Ritter, a specialist in international jurisprudence, pointed out that while he perfectly understood why Lane had walked out, there might be some question as to whether it had been altogether appropriate to have done so. Ritter, after all, was the ambassador. Technically, Lane was part of his staff (in fact, the chief of the interests section was carried on the diplomatic list as a counselor in the Swiss embassy). How, then, could a subordinate walk out in protest while the ambassador remained seated?

Ritter raised the matter not as a reprimand to Lane, but to point to a procedural dilemma that ought to be recognized and discussed. There were conversations about it between Washington and Berne, but as there was obviously no solution to the dilemma, discussion of the matter trailed off inconclusively. What was generally recognized was that the original modus operandi agreed to by all sides created a situation in which the interests section was only *technically* part of the Swiss embassy, but functioned in fact as an independent diplomatic mission. Anomalies were bound to result from such a situation. The chief of the U.S. interests section was regarded as chief of mission and attended official functions in that capacity. That had been accepted as his proper role; and, since it had, he could not behave as if he were in fact a counselor in the Swiss embassy, whatever the title on his calling cards.

The Child Dwarfs the Parent

If succeeding Swiss ambassadors in Havana felt a certain discomfort over having what amounted to an independent American diplomatic mission within the bosom of their own embassy, their discomfort was entirely understandable. When American diplomats had arrived to take over the interests section in 1977, the expectation had been that this would be but a temporary measure, and one which would lead rather quickly to the reestablishment of full diplomatic relations. At the moment of its inception, the United States and Cuba had been intent on ironing out their disagreements. Thus, in agreeing to the establishment of an American-staffed interests section, the Swiss saw themselves in their traditional role as peacemakers. Further, given its supposedly transitional nature, the size of the interests section had been held to a bare minimum—just enough personnel to resume operations on a limited basis.

The situation that in fact evolved, however, was quite different from what had been envisaged. First, it proved impossible for the interests section to operate effectively on an indefinite basis with only ten American employees. Hence, the reciprocal limit was quickly raised to twenty—this with the agreement of the Cuban, Swiss, and Czech governments—and, as time went on, the United States found it necessary to bring in as many as five to ten temporary American personnel at a time. In addition, over a hundred Cubans were employed as support staff. By 1979, the U.S. interests section had become the largest non-Communist diplomatic mission in Havana, dwarfing its parent entity, the Swiss embassy.

Further, it became apparent—especially after the inauguration of Ronald Reagan in January 1981—that there would be no further improvement in U.S.–Cuban relations for many years to come. Quite the contrary, the trend toward renewed tensions, evident since the latter part of 1977, was likely to continue indefinitely. At one point in 1981, there was even reason to believe the United States might take military action against Cuba.

Thus, while the establishment of the interests section had originally been seen as a temporary and organic part of the process of improving relations with Cuba, what it became in fact was a permanent diplomatic link between two bitterly antagonistic governments. To have such an entity even technically within one's own mission was obviously not something which any Swiss ambassador could have contemplated with enthusiasm. Nonetheless, I must say that both ambassadors under whom I served, Jean-Pierre Ritter and (from October 1979) Armin Kamer, bore the situation cheerfully and with the highest degree of professionalism.

During the three years that I was chief of the U.S. interests section, 1979 to 1982, I tried to keep the Swiss ambassador informed of all significant developments related to the interests

section and to U.S.–Cuban relations. He was in an awkward
enough position because of us, I felt; the least we could do was
keep him fully briefed and to consult with him whenever
possible. I am sure it is a practice which has been continued by
all subsequent section chiefs.

The May 2 Incident and Its Aftermath

Despite the efforts of the senior American diplomat to keep the
Swiss ambassador fully informed, the volatility of U.S.–Cuban
relations made for situations that were bound to prove difficult
for all sides. An extreme example of this was the riot in front
of the interests section on May 2, 1980, and the subsequent
period of almost five months during which the section was
home for some four hundred Cubans seeking refuge. All
during that time, it was closed to the public and surrounded by
a police cordon.

The episode began on May 2, during the height of the
Mariel sealift crisis, when some eight hundred former political
prisoners gathered in front of the section to demand to know
when the U.S. government would live up to its promise to
document them for entry into the United States. I went out
front to inform them that the authorization cable had arrived
and that we could begin immediately to call them in on a case-
by-case basis for documentation.

It was dangerous, however, for them to be there, for in
many parts of the city Cuban citizens who expressed an interest
in leaving for the United States were being beaten by their
neighbors. A crowd of eight hundred would-be departees in
front of the interests section was too tempting a target to be
missed for long. I therefore urged the crowd to disperse as
soon as possible. Before they could move off, however, bus-
loads of government supporters arrived and attacked them. A
full-scale riot ensued during which several men were wounded
and possibly one or two killed. More than three hundred of
the former prisoners and more than one hundred men,
women, and children who had been waiting in line for visas
crashed into the building seeking refuge. That afternoon, the

Cuban government offered safe conduct out of the building to any who wished to leave, promising that no one who accepted would be prosecuted or even detained. A few of the refugees accepted (and in fact were not detained), but the great majority continued to fear for their lives and remained within the building. Many of them stayed with us until September.

The Swiss came quickly to our assistance. Ambassador Ritter called the Foreign Ministry on May 2 to express concern and emphasize that the diplomatic immunity of the interests section must be respected. On May 3, he and Mrs. Ritter came to the section to look over the situation and see how they could help us provide for our four hundred guests. They then collected food and medicines from other diplomatic missions and organized a motor convoy system to get these supplies to us. This Swiss "relief service" continued for several days, until we had a chance to organize our own supply system.

On May 17, the Cuban government organized a march past the interests section building during which as many as one million Cubans "demonstrated their repudiation of those who had taken refuge inside." The Cuban government had assured us of adequate police protection (which we got). Even so, with so large a crowd, there was always the possibility that the rowdier elements might get out of hand and attack the building. Ambassador Ritter again stressed to the Cubans the importance of respecting our diplomatic status. Any violation of the interests section, he warned, would be tantamount to an attack on the Swiss embassy itself. To stress that point, he instructed one of his officers to remain inside the section throughout the march and informed the Cubans of this Swiss "presence."

In the event, the May 17 march went smoothly. There were no incidents of any kind. The crowd was orderly, and there were plenty of police on hand to keep them so. Even so, the Swiss presence and support were a reassuring and much appreciated morale booster. On that day, we did not feel ourselves to be only "technically" under the Swiss embassy; rather, we felt ourselves to be very much a part of it.

A few at a time, the refugees inside the section departed. There was never any formal agreement with the Cuban

government guaranteeing their safe departure for the United
States, though government representatives did say they
expected that this would be the outcome in most cases. It was.
As the refugees left the building, all but a handful, who for
reasons of their own could not depart, were permitted to
emigrate to the United States. None was harmed.

No Special Restrictions

No special restrictions, such as travel controls, were imposed
on the staff of the U.S. interests section. These would have
been applied on a reciprocal basis. Since the United States
imposed no such controls on Cuban diplomats in Washington,
the Cubans imposed none on Americans. American personnel
were accorded the same treatment as other diplomatic personnel in Havana.

For all practical purposes, they were also regarded by the
rest of the diplomatic corps as constituting another embassy.
The chief of the U.S. interests section, for example, was invited
to national day receptions and to functions for chiefs of mission
organized by the diplomatic corps as though he were a chargé
d'affaires.

The U.S. Violates the Interests Section Agreement

In their exchange of notes in May of 1977, the United States
and Cuban governments had agreed to treat the chiefs of one
another's interests sections as though they were chiefs of
mission. So far as I know, the Cubans have continued to honor
that agreement. As soon as the Reagan administration came
into office, however, the United States violated it, deciding
unilaterally that henceforth the chief of the Cuban interests
section would not be invited to any more functions given for
chiefs of all missions—functions such as the annual state-of-
the-union address.

This blatant shredding of a key paragraph of an international agreement is to be regretted and, one hopes, will at some
point be corrected.

Conclusions

While the concept of the protecting power is time-worn, interests sections are a recent innovation. Not surprisingly, then, given the limited body of precedent and established procedure, they may be quite different in configuration and purpose—everything from a single diplomat working closely within the embassy of the protecting power to a virtually independent diplomatic mission. The U.S. interests section in Havana represents the latter end of the spectrum. For all practical purposes, it *is* an embassy. It performs all the functions that an embassy would perform. It discusses the same issues with the Cuban government that an embassy would discuss. In some instances, it even discusses them at the same level. Despite the stipulation that the chief of section would only be received at the vice-ministerial level, Lyle Lane, the first section chief, was received once by Castro and several times by the foreign minister. I was received by President Castro, Vice President Carlos Rafael Rodriguez, and Foreign Minister Malmierca many times.

Because of the restrictive attitude of the Reagan administration, and its violation of the agreement regarding treatment of chiefs of section, that has not been the case with my successors. But this has nothing to do with the fact that they head an interests section rather than an embassy. Indeed, under the same circumstances, it is doubtful they would be received at the most senior levels of government even if they were full-fledged ambassadors heading a mission that was an embassy on a de jure, as well as a de facto, basis. Further, during most of the eight-year Reagan administration, the U.S. government had little it wished to discuss with Cuba.

The idea that diplomatic channels do not exist between the United States and Cuba is wrong. The channels exist. Washington simply has not chosen to make full use of them. That tendency, however, began to change toward the end of the Reagan administration, when the United States did negotiate a number of issues with the Cuban government. It also brokered negotiations among Cuba, Angola, and South Africa, which in December of 1988 resulted in a settlement in southern Africa providing for Namibian independence, the withdrawal of South African troops from Angola and Namibia, and the withdrawal of Cuban troops from Angola. The Bush administration, in early 1989, gave evidence of a continued willingness to negotiate its disagreements with Cuba, and possibly even of a disposition to expand the agenda for discussions.

When the United States and Cuba eventually reestablish full diplomatic relations, the only steps that will need to be taken to upgrade the interests section to an embassy will be running up the flag and changing the signs on the door and the chief of mission's desk.

Appendix A

The United States as a Protecting Power, by Country and Date

Illustrative cases in which the United States has served as a protecting power, showing the state(s) represented; the receiving state(s); the duration; and the reason

STATES REPRESENTED: France, Belgium, Britain, Switzerland, Russia, Sweden, Japan, Austria, Prussia, Italy
RECEIVING STATE: Mexico
DURATION: 1867–76
REASON: The overthrow of Austrian Archduke Maximilian by Mexican nationalists led many European states and Japan, which had supported Maximilian's regime, to close their embassies in Mexico and to ask the United States to represent their interests and protect their citizens there. This the United States did, from time to time, for the states listed above. By 1876, these states had all recognized the republican government of General Diaz and reestablished normal relations with Mexico.

STATES REPRESENTED: North German Confederation, Saxony, Hesse, Saxe-Coburg, and Gotha, and later: Colombia, Portugal, Uruguay, the Dominican Republic, Ecuador, Chile, Paraguay, and Venezuela
RECEIVING STATE: France
DURATION: 1870–71
REASON: With the outbreak of the Franco-Prussian War, many German states were represented by the United States in Paris. During the siege of Paris, the United States also represented the Latin states listed above after they had evacuated their embassies.

STATE REPRESENTED: Switzerland
RECEIVING STATES: All states in which Switzerland did not have its own
    representation
DURATION: 1871 and after
REASON: By agreement between the Swiss Federal Council and the
    U.S. State Department, the U.S. government agreed to provide
    "good offices" to Swiss citizens in those countries where the Swiss
    were not represented. This agreement led to the U.S. protection of
    Swiss citizens in China in 1872, Chile in 1885, and Afghanistan in
    1943, among others.

STATE REPRESENTED: Japan
RECEIVING STATE: Hawaii
DURATION: 1871–85
REASON: For the protection of Japanese laborers who decided to stay
    in Hawaii beyond the expiration date of their work visas.

STATE REPRESENTED: Germany
RECEIVING STATE: Guatemala
DURATION: 1874
REASON: The United States agreed to watch over German interests
    until the new German consul could arrive.

STATE REPRESENTED: Italy
RECEIVING STATES: Chile, Peru, and Bolivia
DURATION: 1880
REASON: The U.S. Navy offered to protect Italian citizens on the West
    Coast of South America while Chile and Peru were at war with
    Bolivia. The State Department has no record of any aid actually
    having to be extended, however.

STATE REPRESENTED: China
RECEIVING STATES: Certain American republics
DURATION: 1885–1949
REASON: Beginning with Panama (still part of Colombia in 1885), the
    U.S. instructed its consuls to represent Chinese interests, from time
    to time, where no Chinese representation was present. In 1894,
    protection of Chinese interests was extended to Guatemala and
    Costa Rica; in 1896, to Nicaragua and Salvador; and, in 1941, to
    Colombia, the Dominican Republic, Ecuador, Haiti, Honduras, and
    Venezuela. By 1947, the list had been reduced to only Colombia,
    Ecuador, and Haiti.[1]

STATE REPRESENTED: Japan
RECEIVING STATE: China
DURATION: 1894–95
REASON: The Sino-Japanese War. Reciprocal protection was also granted for Chinese interests in Japan.

STATE REPRESENTED: Britain
RECEIVING STATES: Orange Free State and the Transvaal
DURATION: 1899–1900
REASON: In the first stage of the Boer War (1899–1900), the United States protected British interests and citizens after the British representation was forced to leave Pretoria. In 1900, the Orange Free State and the Transvaal were occupied by British troops, thus negating the necessity of having a protecting power situation.

STATE REPRESENTED: Britain
RECEIVING STATE: Bolivia
DURATION: 1899–1903
REASON: British representatives withdrew from Bolivia after a revolution put in power a government that the British did not recognize until four years later.

STATE REPRESENTED: Japan
RECEIVING STATE: Russia
DURATION: 1904–5
REASON: The Russo-Japanese War. The U.S. was also extensively involved in the repatriation of Japanese prisoners of war.

STATE REPRESENTED: France
RECEIVING STATE: Venezuela
DURATION: 1906–20
REASON: France broke diplomatic relations with Venezuela over the issue of unsettled claims by French citizens against the Venezuelan government. In 1908, the United States also broke relations with Venezuela over unsettled claims by American citizens against the Venezuelan government, producing the unusual situation whereby Brazil protected U.S. interests, though the United States was still officially protecting French interests. The situation was rectified in January 1909 when Brazil was officially recognized by the Venezuelan government as the protecting power for France. Two months later, the United States resumed diplomatic relations with Venezuela and also resumed protection of French interests there. In 1913, France and Venezuela resumed diplomatic relations but the American consul in Maracaibo continued to handle French consular affairs there until 1920.

STATE REPRESENTED: Turkey
RECEIVING STATE: Malta
DURATION: 1914–29

World War I cases[2]
(The following are limited to the protection of diplomatic interests and
do not include protection of consular interests.)

RECEIVING STATE	STATE(S) REPRESENTED	DURATION
Austria-Hungary	France, Britain, Japan	1914–17
	San Marino, Italy	1915–17
Belgium	Austria-Hungary, Denmark, Germany, Britain, Japan, Serbia	1914–17
Britain	Austria-Hungary, Germany, Turkey	1914–17
—in Australia	Austria-Hungary, Germany	1914–17
Bulgaria	Britain	1915–?
Egypt	Brazil, Switzerland	1914–?
	Germany	1914–17
	Austria-Hungary	1915–17
	Salvador	1915–?
France	Austria-Hungary, Germany, Turkey	1914–17
	Guatemala, Nicaragua, Serbia	1914–?
Germany	France (where Spain not in charge), Britain, Canada, Japan, Serbia	1914–17
	San Marino	1915–17
Italy	Norway	1915–?
Japan	Austria-Hungary, Germany	1914–17
	Turkey	1915–17
Liberia	Turkey	1915–17
Morocco	Germany	1914–17
	Austria-Hungary	1915–17
Russia	Germany, Austria-Hungary	1914–17
Serbia	Germany, Austria-Hungary	1914–17
Turkey	Belgium, France (except in Palestine), Britain, Serbia, Switzerland	1914–17
	Italy, Montenegro, Russia, San Marino	1915–17

STATE REPRESENTED: The Netherlands
RECEIVING STATE: Iran
DURATION: 1921–27
REASON: Pending the appointment of a Dutch minister to Iran, the
  United States served as protecting power and took upon itself
  responsibility for protecting Dutch consular interests in Tehran
  after the Dutch consul there died in 1922. The consul was not
  replaced until 1926 and the Dutch ambassador did not arrive until
  1927.

STATE REPRESENTED: Britain
RECEIVING STATE: Honduras
DURATION: 1924

STATE REPRESENTED: Hungary
RECEIVING STATE: Costa Rica
DURATION: 1924–36

STATE REPRESENTED: Italy
RECEIVING STATE: Honduras
DURATION: 1924–25

STATE REPRESENTED: Hungary
RECEIVING STATES: Dominican Republic, Haiti, Honduras
DURATION: 1925

STATE REPRESENTED: Hungary
RECEIVING STATE: Guatemala
DURATION: 1926

STATE REPRESENTED: Britain
RECEIVING STATE: Dominican Republic
DURATION: 1927–28

STATE REPRESENTED: Colombia
RECEIVING STATE: Peru
DURATION: 1933–35

STATE REPRESENTED: Colombia
RECEIVING STATE: Bolivia
DURATION: 1935–36

World War II:

RECEIVING STATE	REPRESENTED STATE(S)	DURATION
Germany	British Empire, Australia, Canada, New Zealand, South Africa	1939–41
	France, Belgium, Luxembourg	1939–40
France (occupied)	Australia, Belgium, British Empire, Canada, Luxembourg, New Zealand, South Africa	1940–41
France (Vichy)	Australia, British Empire, Canada, New Zealand, Belgium, Luxembourg	1940–41
Italy	Australia, Belgium, British Empire, Canada, Egypt, France, New Zealand, Norway, South Africa	1940–41

The U.S. also protected foreign interests in the following states where it maintained a legation but not a full embassy:[3]

Denmark	British Empire, Australia, Canada, South Africa, New Zealand, France, Belgium	1940–41
Bulgaria	British Empire, Canada, New Zealand, Australia, South Africa, Belgium, Netherlands, Yugoslavia, Greece, Luxembourg	1941
Greece	British Empire, Australia, Canada, South Africa, Belgium, Egypt (provisionally)	1941
Hungary	British Empire, Australia, Canada, South Africa, Belgium, New Zealand, Yugoslavia	1941
Rumania	British Empire, Canada, Australia, South Africa, Belgium, Yugoslavia	1941
Yugoslavia	British Empire, New Zealand, Australia, Canada, South Africa, France, Belgium, and provisionally: Egypt and Greece	1941

STATE REPRESENTED: The Philippines
RECEIVING STATES: All states in which the Philippines had not yet
    established formal relations
DURATION: 1946 and after
REASON: Upon obtaining its independence from the United States,
    Manila still depended on the U.S. Foreign Service to represent it in
    countries where no independent Philippine representation existed.

STATE REPRESENTED: Britain
RECEIVING STATE: Yemen Arab Republic (North Yemen)
DURATION: 1963–67
REASON: Yemeni Civil War (War of Revolution).

Appendix B

Protecting Powers That Have Represented the United States, by Country and Date

Illustrative cases in which the United States has been a protected power, showing the protecting power, the receiving state(s), the duration, and the reason.

PROTECTING POWER: Brazil
RECEIVING STATE: Venezuela
DURATION: 1908–9
REASON: At issue in the diplomatic break with Venezuela were the unsettled claims of American citizens against the Venezuelan government.

U.S. Involvement in World War I:
DURATION: April 1917–November 1918

PROTECTING POWER	RECEIVING STATE(S)
Spain	Austria-Hungary, Belgium, Germany
Sweden	Turkey

PROTECTING POWER: Switzerland
RECEIVING STATES: Bulgaria, Denmark, Germany, Hungary, Italy, Japan; occupied: China, France, Rumania, and Thailand
DURATION: December 1941–September 1945
REASON: U.S. involvement in World War II

PROTECTING POWER: Switzerland
RECEIVING STATE: Bulgaria
DURATION: 1950–58
REASON: The United States broke relations after a series of Bulgarian
affronts culminating in their declaring the U.S. minister persona
non grata

PROTECTING POWER: Switzerland
RECEIVING STATE: Cuba
DURATION: 1961–present
REASON: The break in U.S.–Cuban relations was sparked by Castro's
demand that the U.S. embassy in Havana reduce its staff from
nearly 300 to only 11, which the United States refused to do.

Aftermath of the June 1967 Arab-Israeli War:

PROTECTING POWER	RECEIVING STATE	DURATION
Belgium	Iraq	1967–84
Italy	Yemen Arab Republic	1967–72
	Syria	1967–74
Netherlands	The Sudan	1967–72
Spain	Egypt	1967–74
	Mauritania	1967–70
Switzerland	Algeria	1967–74

PROTECTING POWER: Switzerland
RECEIVING STATE: Iran
DURATION: 1980–present
REASON: As a result of the Iranian hostage crisis

PROTECTING POWER: Belgium
RECEIVING STATE: Libya
DURATION: 1980–present
REASON: Relations were broken off by the Reagan administration due
to Libya's alleged ties to terrorist organizations.

PROTECTING POWER: United Kingdom
RECEIVING STATE: People's Democratic Republic of Yemen (former
British Protectorate of Aden)
DURATION: 1969–present
REASON: The government of the PDRY severed ties with Washington
after a radical faction of the ruling National Liberation Front
assumed power in Aden in October 1969.

NOTE

There are no available records of formal third-party protection of U.S. interests in the Soviet Union between 1918 and 1933 or in the People's Republic of China between 1949 and the opening of the U.S. liaison office in Beijing in 1973.

Additionally, in the following countries the United States has no diplomatic relations and its interests have been protected by no third power:

Albania—Since 1939
Kampuchea—Since 1975
North Korea—Not recognized by the United States
Vietnam—Since 1975. (The United States does not recognize the communist government in Hanoi. Legislation on Capitol Hill calling for the reciprocal establishment of Vietnamese and American interests sections in Washington and Hanoi was introduced by Sen. John McCain (R–Arizona) [S. CON. RES. 109, March 24, 1988] and Rep. Thomas Ridge (R–Pennsylvania) [H. CON. RES. 271, March 23, 1988]. Neither bill was acted upon.)

Notes

1. The Origins and Use of the Protecting Power

1. Garrett Mattingly, *Renaissance Diplomacy* (Baltimore: Penguin Books, Inc., 1964), pp. 10, 65–70. [First published 1955 by Houghton, Mifflin (Boston) and Cape (London).]

2. William McHenry Franklin, *Protection of Foreign Interests: A Study in Diplomatic and Consular Practice* (Washington, D.C.: U.S. Government Printing Office, 1947), pp. 8 *et seq.* [hereafter, Franklin]. This study prepared under the auspices of the Special Projects Division of the Department of State is based on broad research into the primary sources on the subject. Although it is written primarily out of the experience of the United States, it is rich in detail regarding the experience of other countries that have served as protecting powers. The study remains a guide not only for American diplomatic officers but also for any writers on the subject, and this essay draws on it extensively.

3. Marjorie M. Whiteman, "Diplomatic Missions and Embassy Property, Protection of Interests by Third States," *Digest of International Law* (Washington, D.C.: U.S. Government Printing Office, 1970), pp. 450–51.

4. Franklin, pp. 118–19.

5. Ibid., pp. 39–44. See also P. Dougherty, *American Diplomats and the Franco-Prussian War: Perceptions from Paris and Berlin* (Washington, D.C.: Institute for the Study of Diplomacy, Georgetown University, 1981).

6. Ibid., p. 45.

7. Ibid., p. 49.

8. Department of State, *Foreign Affairs Manual*, Vol. 7, November 3, 1986, Ch. 1000, App. A, "Protection of Foreign Interests," ¶924.2: Restrictions on Actions, pp. 3–4.

9. Franklin, pp. 69–73, 78–79, 96–99, 102–3, 219.

10. Whiteman, p. 455. The extent to which an American interests section

could come to be regarded as a *de facto* diplomatic mission, particularly within the local diplomatic corps, has been reflected by occasional references to its head as "the American chargé d'affaires." An American officer who served for several months as head of an interests section in an Arab country that had severed diplomatic relations with the United States recalls being introduced in that way to a foreign dignitary on a public occasion. A senior officer of the host country's Protocol Office who was also present overheard the introduction and immediately interjected that the American officer was not the American chargé d'affaires but "the chief of the American services section," the term "services" being the preferred usage of the Foreign Ministry. The protocol official was of course correct, inasmuch as there were no diplomatic relations between the United States and his country.

11. Whiteman, pp. 454–55.

12. The information on the organization, staffng, and structure of the U.S. interests sections is drawn from material provided by the Office of the Historian of the Department of State; from Whiteman (cited above); and from conversations with personnel who were assigned to those sections. Part II of this book provides detailed accounts of several such sections.

13. The nature of the protecting power arrangement with Switzerland for Iran is set forth in a *procès-verbal* of May 12, 1980; that with respect to Belgium regarding Libya is in a *procès-verbal* of August 12, 1982.

14. John Boyd, Ed., *Digest of United States Practice in International Law 1977* (Washington: U.S. Department of State, 1983), pp. 22–25.

15. United Nations Conference on Diplomatic Intercourse and Immunities, Vienna, Austria, March 2–April 14, 1961. *Report of the Delegation of the United States of America with related documents*, Department of State Publication 7289 (Washington, D.C., February 1962), p.49. See also Article 8 of the 1963 Vienna Convention on Consular Relations (United Nations, *Treaty Series*, vol. 596, pp. 261ff.).

2. The "Good Offices" of Switzerland

1. The 1872 settlement by a neutral tribunal in Geneva of U.S. claims against Britain of $15,500,000—for direct losses caused by the *Alabama* and other ships launched from British territory—was notable for the new impetus it gave to the process of arbitration in the peaceful settlement of international disputes.

2. In 1889 the Portuguese government's seizure of the railway, constructed under a concession granted to an American citizen, led to representations by the governments of the United States and Great Britain (representing British investors in the venture). Portugal agreed to submit the claim for indemnity to arbitration by three jurists chosen by the president of Switzerland.

3. War was averted when the Chilean government agreed to pay an indemnity of $75,000 to the families of the killed and wounded seamen, despite Chile's insistence that the seamen were to blame.

4. Since the middle of the last century, the institution of the protecting power has gradually become established as customary law and is now partly embodied in Articles 45 and 46 of the 1961 Vienna Convention on Diplomatic Relations, as noted by James Blake in chapter 1, as well as in Article 8 of the 1963 Vienna Convention on Consular Relations (the Geneva Red Cross Conventions of 1949 and their Additional Protocol I of 1977 pertaining to the humanitarian function of the protecting power being disregarded in the present context).

5. David D. Newsom, "The Sensitive Link: The Swiss Role in the U.S.–Iran Hostage Crisis," in *Einblick in die schweizerische Außenpolitik*, Verlag Neue Zürcher Zeitung, 1984.

6. Harold H. Saunders, "Diplomacy under Pressure (November 1979– May 1980)" and "Beginning of the End," in *American Hostages in Iran: The Conduct of a Crisis*, by Warren Christopher et al., a Council on Foreign Relations Book (New Haven: Yale University Press, 1985).

3. The Swiss Role in the U.S.–Iran Hostage Crisis

1. U.S. Congress, House of Representatives, Committee on Foreign Affairs, *Iran's Seizure of the U.S. Embassy, Hearings*, February 19, 1981.

4. Evacuation and Hand-over: Baghdad, 1967

1. *The Yearbook of the United Nations, 1967*, published in 1969 by the UN Office of Public Information in New York, and the *Middle East Journal* 21:4 (Autumn 1967) have refreshed my memory and filled out details on the Security Council debates.

2. *Middle East Journal* 21:4, p. 503.

3. The account of the Security Council debates is from *The Yearbook of the United Nations 1967*, pp. 176–78.

4. "Night action" messages signify the need for immediate action, whether night or day.

5. Conversation April 25, 1987, with Ambassador Parker T. Hart, chief of mission in Ankara in 1967.

6. It is sad to have to relate that Ambassador Dupret was to perish a few years later, while ambassador to Morocco, in an attempted coup against the Moroccan monarchy. The palace in Rabat was attacked during a reception attended by the king and many foreign ambassadors. In writing to his widow, I recalled the special gratitude and affection in which his American friends had held him, stemming partly from his forthright actions in 1967.

5. Under the Flag of Spain, Cairo, 1967–1974

1. The word "households" was proposed by the Egyptians. They defined it as "butler, major domo, or person having to do with security."—D. C. B.

8. The Protecting Power and the U.S. Interests Section in Cuba

1. From April 21 to September 26, 1980, over 125,000 Cubans left Cuba for Florida by boat from Mariel Harbor following Castro's announcement of safe conduct for would-be emigrants who had taken refuge in the Peruvian embassy in Havana or were relatives of Cuban-Americans.

Appendix A, The United States as a Protecting Power

1. In William McHenry Franklin, *Protection of Foreign Interests: A Study in Diplomatic and Consular Practice* (Washington, D.C.: U.S. Government Printing Office, 1947), Appendix III, "Partial List of Foreign Interests Protected by the United States...between the World Wars," pp. 257–60, there are conflicts at some points with the information found in the text, though this may be due to China's breaking off and then resuming its use of the United States as a protecting power in a given country (i.e., the text indicates that the United States served as the protecting power for China in Guatemala in 1894, while the appendix shows that relationship beginning in 1920).

2. Franklin also notes that the U.S. represented Rumanian interests at many posts, after that state became a belligerent, and protected Turkey in Mexico, although no dates are specified for either case.

3. Also note Franklin's appendices V, "Foreign Interests Relinquished by the United States to Switzerland in December 1941," pp. 266–68; VI, "Foreign Interests Protected by the United States as of January 1944," pp. 269–71; and VII, "Powers Protecting Enemy Interests in the United States during World War II," p. 272.

Index